The Path:
Family Storybook

A Journey through the
Bible for Families

Lindsay Hardin Freeman

and

Melody Wilson Shobe

~

Illustrations by Roger Speer

© 2016 Forward Movement

All rights reserved.

ISBN: 9780880284394

Printed in USA

Forward
Movement

The Path:
Family Storybook

A Journey through the
Bible for Families

Lindsay Hardin Freeman and Melody Wilson Shobe

Illustrations by Roger Speer

Forward Movement

Cincinnati, Ohio

Table of Contents

Dear Reader,

It's good to see you here. Welcome!

Have you ever been to a family reunion? If so, perhaps your grandparents and great-grandparents were there. You might have hugged them or heard stories about when they grew up. Or perhaps you've never met those people. Perhaps they died before you were born, or they live in a faraway place.

Think of this book as a big family reunion of your ancestors, your spiritual ancestors. Just as important as people to whom you are biologically related, spiritual ancestors are people who lived before us and whose lives of faith helped shape our lives.

Here, you will be part of their stories.

Ride the ark with Noah and his family, and see otters and iguanas scamper down the gangplank after ten long months of being cooped up together. Watch Deborah ride out on horseback, leading 10,000 soldiers into battle. Learn about Samson and how he lost his strength after his famous haircut—and how he died a hero. And stand with the shepherds and angels around Jesus' manger on the most brilliant day of all.

People in the Bible may seem like they lived ages ago. What, you might wonder, do you have in common with people who lived before there were cell phones or electricity or computers or cars?

The answer: Lots. Your spiritual ancestors stood tall against those who tried to hurt them; they fell in love, and they became mothers and fathers. They went to war, they battled illnesses, and they told stories about how God helped them through terrible times.

This book, like the Bible, is a collection of the stories that our ancestors told their children and grandchildren around the fire and when they tucked their little ones into bed each night. These are the memories that kept them strong when they were scared and gave them reason to celebrate when they remembered the happy times.

You stand in this line of people who love God. You stand in this line of people who gathered around Jesus and became his followers.

Wrap up in their stories like you would with a blanket around your shoulders. By doing so, they will become your stories. Bundle up in these memories. Snuggle into them. Count on their warmth and comfort during cold days. In doing so, you'll weave the people of God into your life, and you'll hold them tightly on your heart—just as God holds you.

In Christ,

Lindsay Hardin Freeman
Melody Wilson Shobe

The Path: Family Storybook can be used as part of a Christian formation program called *Living Discipleship: Exploring the Bible*, which also includes a youth and adult version called *The Path: A Journey through the Bible*. Another resource, an all-ages coloring book called *Pathways of Faith*, is a wonderful companion as well.

Living Discipleship: Exploring the Bible takes participants on a journey through the scriptures, from Genesis to Revelation. One of the main ways that we know and understand the hope to which God has called us is the gift of God's Word, the Bible. By focusing on the vast narrative of the scriptures, we can see the great story of God's love from the beginning of creation, through the life of Jesus Christ, and in our own time, guided by the Holy Spirit. Through the stories of scripture, we can learn that the hope God offered to the faithful in ages past is the very same hope God is offering us today.

Facilitator's guides for the family storybook and for the youth and adult version are available for teachers and leaders at www.ForwardMovement.org. Additional resources can be found at www.LivingDiscipleship-FM.org.

Exploring the Bible is part of a three-year, all-ages curriculum designed to help individuals and communities know more fully God revealed in Christ Jesus. *Living Discipleship* is structured in three years: one year on *Exploring the Bible*, one year on *Celebrating the Saints*, and one year on *Practicing our Faith*. *Living Discipleship* is a tool for churches and leaders, a resource for helping Christians come to know the hope, the glorious inheritance, and the immeasurable power of the risen Christ.

To learn more, visit www.LivingDiscipleship-FM.org.

Creation: You are There!

Based on Genesis 1:1-31

Should you choose to accept the following mission, you will hear and see something amazing. Today, your task is to imagine being at God's side for the very first days of creation. It's easy to take God's world for granted. We go to sleep at night and we wake up in the morning. Shining in the sky every day is the sun, and waltzing across the night sky each evening is the moon.

But what if there were no sun or stars? No people. No earth. Nothing. That's what it was like for God a long, long time ago. Nothing breathed or scampered or ran or sang or even cried because there was nothing but God. Nothing.

And God wanted more than emptiness.

God wanted people because God has a huge heart. God wanted to watch whales frolic in the sea. God wanted frisky otters to slide down rocks and chase each other across beautiful streams. God wanted hot deserts and shimmering ice caps.

Picture yourself in those dark days, standing next to God, in that vast darkness. Remember there is nothing to see, nothing to hear. Suddenly, you hear a simple command: **"Let there be light!"**

In that moment, the gloom rolls away, and you are surrounded by beautiful, magnificent light—light that reaches up and twists away from the darkness, separating itself.

"Let this darkness be called Night, and this light be called Day," God says.

You have witnessed the first day of creation. Wow. But somehow you're a bit tired. You close your eyes and sleep, nuzzled into God's side; when you wake up early the next day, God is just getting started.

"Look over there," God says. **"Look where it is dark and murky. Look where the earth is covered with nothing but water. Let there be a firmament in the midst of waters, and let it separate the waters from the waters."**

What? Separate the waters from the waters? What does that mean? And then you realize that the ocean and sky are taking shape before your eyes. God is turning chaos into something firm, something you can see and touch and smell. Both sea and sky are huge; they reach as far as you can see, farther than you can imagine. Once again, you sleep.

Progress continues. The next morning, on the third day, you hear God's strong and tender voice: **"Let the waters under the sky be gathered together into one place, and let the dry land appear."** From the murky depths of the ocean emerge amazing land forms: mountains, rivers, hills, deserts, plains, lakes, volcanoes, and glaciers. Colors spring up before your eyes as trees and plants begin to dot the landscape.

Apples fall from trees. Dandelion seeds blow into the wind. Pomegranates and watermelons sprout before your eyes.

One day turns into another, and soon it is the fourth day. You look up and see the sun, its beautiful, blazing rays shining to light the day. God has put it there just this moment, set in the sky to mark days and seasons and years. And as the fourth day passes into night, God shapes the moon and flings stars across the great black expanse of sky. As the moon and stars twinkle with delight, you are comforted by the light shining through the darkness, and you fall asleep full of joy.

The morning of the fifth day brings a lovely surprise: you look at where God is pointing—the oceans—and they are strangely silent. And then you see great whales leaping and breaching and jumping. Birds are cawing and hooting and kerfuffling, and the skies are soon full of eagles and hawks and tiny little chickadees. Once again, you snuggle down by God's side to sleep.

The sixth day comes, and you wonder what God will create. The skies and the waters are teeming with life, but the land is quiet and empty. Then suddenly all around you see cows and sheep and goats. And over the horizon peek the long, sloping necks of giraffes, the giant flapping ears of elephants, the scaly, shining skin of chameleons. You have taken them for granted before but no longer. Bleating and mooing and snorting fill your ears. This is fun!

But God is not done, for there seems to be something missing. You hear God sigh, much like you do when something isn't quite right. And then you wonder: Could God be lonely, in spite of all the signs of life around you?

In that moment, God gently scoops some dirt from the earth and blows on it with the breath of God's spirit. You gasp with wonder as you see what God has made: two human beings, man and woman. You watch as they take their first breath of the bracing, clean air.

"Take good care of everything that I have made." says God. **"And be fruitful and multiply; the earth is to be filled and treated lovingly, as I would do."**

You awake early the next morning to sounds of life. God looks at you, and you look back, somehow knowing that today is a day of rest, both for God and for you. Today, there will be no activity on God's part except to love you and all of creation. And that is enough.

It is more than enough, and you give thanks, remembering these words: **"This is the day that the Lord has made: Let us rejoice and be glad in it!"**

Reflection Questions

- What comes to your mind when you visualize God creating the earth and all that is in it?

- What is your favorite part of creation? Do you think God might have a favorite part? What might that be?

- Why is it important to know that God rested on the seventh day? What might that say to us?

- God so loved this world and continues to love it. God asks human beings to love and care for the world. How can you help God take care of creation?

Noah & the Ark:
Riding the Waves!

Based on Genesis 6-9

I t's hard to keep anything bright and shiny for long, and that's what it was like with creation. As much as God wanted everything to run smoothly in this new creation, there were some problems, almost from the start.

Adam and Eve, the first man and the first woman, made a mess of things. Surrounded by lush beauty and peace, they broke the one rule that God had given them: Don't eat the fruit from the Tree of Life. Sadly, they didn't listen, reaching out and munching on that fruit like it was a giant candy bar. God ordered them out of paradise, out of the beautiful Garden of Eden that he had so lovingly made.

Things soon went from bad to worse. Fights broke out between Adam and Eve's children. One of their boys, Cain, actually killed his brother, Abel. Other relatives fought without end. Meanness, stealing, and murder seemed to have taken over.

God's heart was broken. Somewhere between sadness and anger, he vowed to rid the earth of human beings and animals.

"I will destroy my own creation!" God said. **"I will destroy the human beings, as well as the animals and creeping things and birds of the air, for I am sorry that I have made them."**

Ouch. Even the stars winced. God had never talked like this before. Everyone—everything—seemed to hold their breath...waiting...waiting...to see what he would do.

Sighing, God's eyes roamed up and down the earth. Was there anything good in all of creation? Were human beings beyond hope? Was it a good idea to have created them in the first place, to have given them freedom to make their own decisions?

And then God saw a man whom he knew to be good: Noah. Like a calm lake in the midst of spine-crackling thunderstorms, Noah peacefully went about life. He worked, and he prayed, and he loved his family—and they loved him.

I can't destroy Noah, thought God. *Noah is what I had in mind when I created human beings: good, strong, healthy, and able to turn away from evil. Noah is righteous.*

"**Noah,**" said God. "**Listen up. I have to make a few adjustments to my original plan. There's lots of trouble out there, and I need you to help me straighten things out.**

"**You and your family will be saved, but I am going to have a flood destroy much of what I made. So build a big ark for you and your family and make sure they are safe on the ark. Then take pairs, mating pairs, male and female, of all the animals and birds and reptiles on the earth, every living thing, and put them on the boat with you.**"

Whew, thought Noah. *That's a big order. Build a boat? A huge boat?? Put two of every kind of animal and bug and bird and reptile on the boat and sail away? And watch the earth flood?*

Being the good man he was, however, Noah got right to work, following God's surprisingly detailed plans about how to build the ark. "**The length is to be three hundred cubits...its breadth fifty cubits...its height thirty cubits...make a roof for the ark...put the door high up in the side...make a first, second, and third deck.**"

Years and years went by, but Noah faithfully continued working. Noah was 600 years old when the ark was finally ready. And then, after Noah loaded two of every living thing into their own cages and burrows and stalls and stables, God began to flood the earth. All the creatures left in the flood waters drowned. But Noah and his family lived, as did the chickens and horses and beetles and pandas and moose that rode along in the ark, clucking and neighing and bellowing and snorting.

For forty days and nights, it rained and rained. Sealed tightly, the great boat slowly rose until it sailed on top of waters that were even higher than the tallest mountains on the earth.

Month after month, like a surfer riding the waves, the ark rode the water. Finally, at the end of ten months, the ark came to rest on the mountains of Ararat. Opening a tiny porthole, Noah sent one of his two doves to see if land could be found. The exhausted dove flew and flew, but it found no land, so the dove returned to Noah's outstretched hand. Seven days later, Noah sent the dove out again—and this time it returned with an olive branch in its beak. Signs of life! In seven more days, Noah sent the dove out again. And this time it did not return, for it had found dry land on which to perch.

"**Come out of the ark, Noah!**" God said. "**And let everyone else out, too, your family and all those animals that have been cooped up for so long.**"

Thrilled to be free, Noah's family glided down the ark's ramp. Then came all the animals and bees and fish, snorting and slithering and gallumphing, finding their new home in water and on land and in the skies. Finally, Noah, captain of the ship, came last. His job—to bring all of God's creation to safety—was done. And God had a surprise for Noah and his family, one that thrilled and delighted them.

"Look in the sky," God said. "It is there that I have set my bow as a sign that never again will I destroy the earth with flooding waters. I give you my word, and the rainbow is a sign of the Covenant that unites us. You are safe, and I will always watch out for you and every living creature of every kind that is found on the earth."

Reflection Questions

- Why does God choose Noah and his family to survive the flood? What about them is different?

- How do you think Noah and his family feel while they are on the ark? How do you think the animals feel?

- What does God want us to think about when we see a rainbow? Why is that important?

Abraham & Sarah:
On Their Way to the Promised Land

Based on Genesis 12 and 18

After Noah and his family and all the animals left the ark and built new homes, the earth buzzed with life. Many years went by, and God loved his creation more than ever. God had particular affection for a man named Abraham, an owner of sheep and goats. Although they did not know it at the time, Abraham and his wife, Sarah, would be the primary ancestors of many, including Jewish and Christian people. Through Abraham and Sarah, God would bring his people to their own land, the Promised Land.

Abraham stared up into the darkening sky, for dusk was his favorite time. He took the same walk every night, looking for his friends, the stars. Each night they appeared like laundry on a clothesline, washing themselves across the sky, swinging in the breeze. Abraham knew the stars by name, as if they were family. Like relatives around the dinner table, they were always a bit different each night yet always present, always beloved.

Other men had children and grandchildren to share their table. Most had great-grandchildren. But Abraham and his wife Sarah, despite many prayers, had remained childless. And now, Abraham was 75. Sarah was 65. Much too old to have babies. Soon their years would come to an end, and their bodies would be buried alongside their ancestors in the desert sand.

From the hillside, Abraham saw homes turn dark, one by one, as oil lamps were extinguished below him. Like the stars after a night of work, homes were bright one minute and subdued the next. Children were tucked in. Voices of love wafted through the air. Sounds of family.

Time for sleep, he thought. Old men may not sleep as soundly as those who are young, but they still need to rest. And then, as he did every night, he gave one more look to his star friends. "Good night," he said. "Good night."

But the stars had gone dim. The moon, present just seconds ago, had also disappeared. Did the sky know something he didn't? And then he heard an indescribably tender yet strong voice.

"Abraham."

What? The old man glanced about, looking for who might be speaking, but he was alone.

"Go from your country and your kindred to the land that I will show you. I will make of you a great nation, and I will bless you."

Abraham was sure he must be hearing things. *What? No, it can't be... Was it...? No, I'll just hurry and get back home to Sarah.* The voice rang out again, even stronger.

"Go from your country and your kindred to the land that I will show you. I will make of you a great nation, and I will bless you."

In that moment, Abraham knew. Without question, it was God's voice!

At once, the old man fell on his knees. Hearing God's voice was an honor too great for words. And what God said seemed almost incomprehensible. A great nation would mean children and grandchildren. A great nation would mean a full table at home and a land full of descendants, both for Abraham and for God.

Racing home, words bubbled from his lips. **"Children! Grandchildren! A great nation! We must do as God says! We must leave home at once!"**

Sarah flew into action. Within days, she packed their things and prepared food for the journey. With servants, relatives, sheep, goats, camels, and tents, the caravan set out. Climbing mountains and crossing deserts is not easy at any age. But in those days, travel was especially hard. There were no doctors, no antibiotics, no ambulances to help if someone should break a leg or experience a heart attack.

Yet Abraham and Sarah trusted God. They had done as he had asked. Based on God's word, they expected children. Lots of them. Month after month went by. *Surely,* thought Sarah, *I will be pregnant soon.* Yet nothing happened. Year after year went by. Nothing. Decades followed, with no sign of a child.

And then, when all seemed lost, three men came to visit Abraham and Sarah. One day they just appeared. Abraham and Sarah offered the guests their very best hospitality, cooking a young goat. As was the custom then, the men shared the meal together, while the women prepared the food behind a tent wall.

"This time next year," said one of the men, **"when we come back, Sarah will have a son in her arms."**

What? Listening behind the tent wall, Sarah started to laugh to herself. She would soon be ninety years old, much too old to have babies. *What was the man thinking? And how could he know?*

And then came the voice again from the other side of the tent.

"Why did your wife laugh just now?"

Oh, no. They had heard.

She laughed because what they said seemed impossible. But nothing is impossible with God. The men who had appeared, as if coming out of the desert sand, were actually angels. And the one who had promised children to Abraham all those years ago was none other than God.

And God keeps his promises.

A year later, Sarah and Abraham finally had their son. They named him Isaac, which means "laughter."

Isaac grew to be a good and holy man. He married Rebekah, and they had two sons, Jacob and Esau. And his sons had sons and daughters, and their children had sons and daughters.

Abraham's small family was the beginning of a multitude of people, God's people, later known as the Hebrew people, the Israelite nation. Today they are known as the Jewish people. From Abraham and Sarah came the ancestors of Jesus, the ancestors of you and me, fellow children in the family of God. Today, the ancestors of Abraham number more than the stars in the sky, more than the grains of sand in the desert, just as God promised all those years ago.

Reflection Questions

- The word "ancestor" means all the people who have gone before us, like our grandparents and great-grandparents. Who are your ancestors?

- Abraham and Sarah and other people in the Bible are what we call our spiritual ancestors. Why are they important to us?

- What do you think the guests who showed up at Abraham's tent looked like? Do you think they were people? Or angels? Or God?

- Abraham heard God's voice many times. What do you think God's voice sounded like? Have you ever heard God's voice? What was it like?

Sometimes terrible things happen, things that make our stomachs hurt and our hearts break. Yet what we don't always remember is that God sees these bad things and uses them for good.

That's what happened long ago in the ancient land of Canaan, where a boy named Joseph lived with his eleven brothers and their father, Jacob. Ten of those brothers were older than Joseph, and one, Benjamin, was younger. Benjamin and Joseph's mother was Rachel, and the other brothers were born from a different mother, Leah.

Sometimes siblings don't get along, and that was surely the case in Joseph's family. What made things worse was that Joseph was their father's favorite son. One day Jacob gave Joseph a beautiful, long-sleeved coat. Like a boiling pot on the stove, jealousy simmered. None of the brothers had anything like the coat.

Joseph did not help the situation much, as he would often complain to his father about his brothers. And sometimes Joseph would tell his brothers about dreams in which they would bow down to him.

"I had a dream in which we were all binding sheaves of wheat!" Joseph told them. "My sheaf rose up and stood upright, and I saw your sheaves gather round and bow to mine!" Then, "I've had another dream! I saw the sun and moon and eleven stars bowing to me."

Everyone, including his father, was unhappy with him. "A fine dream to have! All of us, including me, your mother, AND your brothers are to come and bow down before you?"

Tensions grew in the family. One day, the ten older brothers, now grown men, were tending the family sheep at Shechem (SHEE-kuhm), a nearby town, when Jacob sent Joseph to check on his brothers.

Seeing Joseph coming, wearing his special coat, their anger flared. "There's that troublemaker! There's that man of dreams! Let's kill him!" And they meant it.

Reuben, the oldest brother, tried to stop things. "No! Shed no blood. We must not take his life. Throw him in that well over there instead, while we have lunch and figure things out. "

You can imagine the conversation. *What should we do with Joseph? If we pull him out of the well, he'll tell Dad what happened. And if we kill him? Even WE know how wrong that is.*

Judah, one of the brothers, had an idea. "What do we get by killing him? Let's not hurt him but sell him as a slave instead." A few minutes later, for twenty pieces of silver, Joseph was tied up, shackled, and carted off to lands unknown.

To make it look like he had been killed by wild animals, the brothers dipped Joseph's beautiful coat in goat's blood. And because cowards do not like to look people in the eye, they sent the coat home to their father by messenger. Jacob was heartbroken and mourned for his son for a very long time. What he did not know was that Joseph was alive and had been taken to Egypt, and there, his ability to interpret dreams would come in handy.

One day, during a stint in jail for a crime he did not commit, Joseph was called out of prison. Pharaoh had a dream he could not understand.

"I dreamt I was standing on the banks of the Nile River," Pharaoh told Joseph. "Seven cows, fat and sleek, came up out of the Nile and began to eat. And then seven scrawny cows came up after them and ate up all the fat cows but looked as thin as when they started. Then I woke up."

"Your dream is clear," said Joseph. "The seven fat cows mean seven years of plenty for Egypt. Crops will grow, and we will flourish. But after seven years, there will be a horrible famine, and everyone will go hungry. You need to choose a man who is intelligent and wise to govern Egypt. Save some of the corn and other grains. Tuck them away so that you will have food for all the people during the seven years of famine."

Pharaoh realized that Joseph was a wise and intelligent man. "Since God has shown you all this, there is no one so discerning and wise as you...I am giving you authority over the land of Egypt. People shall respect your orders; only this throne shall set me above you."

Just as Pharaoh had hoped, Joseph was a wise steward. Egypt flourished. But those years of famine crept up. Soon many, including Joseph's father and brothers and their families back in Canaan, were starving. Hearing that grain was for sale in Egypt, Jacob sent his sons to speak to the man in charge. "Go buy some for us, that we may survive and not die." Little did they know that that the man in charge was Joseph, the brother they had sold into slavery.

Picture the moment. Talk about awkward. The brothers did not recognize Joseph, but he remembered them. And, at first, he took revenge.

"Where did you come from?" he barked.

"From Canaan, to buy food."

"You are spies!"

And with that, Joseph locked up his brothers for three days—but not before learning that their youngest brother was still at home with their father. "If you want food, go home and bring that brother here!" he told them.

Jacob, the boy's father, was overjoyed to see his sons. When they explained the plan to him, he refused to send Benjamin, for he had come to love the young boy almost as much as he had loved Joseph. Yet the famine was too great, the hunger too strong, and soon, Jacob relented.

When they returned, Joseph played one last trick on his brothers. He had a silver cup placed into Benjamin's bag, making Benjamin look like a thief. When the cup was discovered, the brothers were horrified, fearing they would be thrown in jail forever. But Joseph's love for his brothers and father overcame any further thoughts of revenge. Seeing Benjamin, Joseph wept so loudly that even those outside the palace could hear him.

"I am Joseph! Is my father really still alive?" he asked. Stunned, his brothers could not answer. "Do not be afraid. It was not you who sent me here but God, so that I could save your lives." And throwing his arms around Benjamin, he wept, kissed his brothers, and forgave them.

"The evil you planned to do to me has by God's design been turned to good, that he might bring about, as indeed he has, the deliverance of a numerous people."

Joseph and his family went on to be a great people in the land of Egypt.... until years later there arose a Pharaoh "who knew not Joseph."

But that's another story.

Reflection Questions

- What do you think Joseph's special coat looked like? Have you ever gotten a special present from someone? What was it? How did it make you feel?

- Joseph had many special dreams that told him things about God and the world. How do you think Joseph knew what his dreams meant? What do you dream about?

- Joseph told his brothers that God had used their bad behavior to do good things. How does God still do that? Are there times when your bad behavior led to something good?

Moses: Let My People Go!

Based on Exodus 1-12

Joseph governed Egypt for many years, and his family lived peacefully in the country. Eventually, however, a new Pharaoh came to power who did not know Joseph or his family. The Israelites were forced into slavery, and the people worked night and day, suffering greatly. In that land, though, lived a girl whose good deed would make a difference for years to come.

The day dawned beautiful and bright—a perfect day to be outside. Armed with fluffy white linens and kind servants, Pharaoh's daughter set out on one of her favorite walks: the path to the Nile River. Winding away from the palace and through tall bulrushes, she knew to steer clear of shallow spots in which crocodiles might be hiding, ready to snap.

She glanced back at the palace, wondering if she might spot her father at the window, waving, as he had often done when she was younger. *No. He's too busy lately, full of worries. It's almost as if he's become someone else. So troubled, so angry…so scary.* Just last week, Pharaoh issued a terrible order: that all Hebrew male babies under the age of two be killed. She had heard the palace guards talking under her window about the terrible order.

Shuddering, the girl felt grateful to be near the calm, sun-splashed water. But as she approached the water's edge, she noticed something. A basket floated in the water, a hand-woven basket…and it was rocking, shifting, moving…on its own? Racing into the water, the girl threw open the basket's top. She gasped. Looking right at her was a baby! Dark-haired, brown-eyed, and red-cheeked, the infant immediately reached for the girl's long, black hair.

Pharaoh's daughter knew the truth. "This is a Hebrew baby!"

With one word from her, the baby would die. Her father would be proud. The servants standing on the banks were speechless. And then a single voice rang out: "Shall I go and find you a nurse among the Hebrew women to feed the child?"

Turning around, Pharaoh's daughter spotted a girl about her own age.

"Yes," she replied. "By all means. I will pay the nurse. And once the child is weaned, bring him back to the palace, where he can grow up, and I will take care of him. I will call him Moses, for I drew him up out of the water."

Pharaoh's daughter was brave and did the right thing. The girl at the riverbank was Miriam, Moses' sister. She and Moses' mother had taken a huge risk by putting the baby in the river. They hoped and prayed that someone would save the boy's life—and Pharaoh's daughter had answered their prayers!

As Moses grew, he witnessed the terrible abuse of his people. Used as slaves to build roads and bridges and quarries and pyramids, the Hebrew people (also known as the Israelites) were routinely tortured and beaten by the Egyptians, under Pharaoh's orders.

One day, things got so bad that Moses ran away from Egypt. But he couldn't run away from God. In the middle of the desert, Moses saw a strange bush. The bush was covered in flames, but it did not burn up! Moses turned aside to see this amazing sight, and as he got near the bush, he heard a voice that echoed through his bones. The voice was loud and tender at the same time.

"Moses, Moses," said the voice.

"Here I am," Moses replied, his own voice shaking.

The voice spoke again, "I am the God of your father, the God of Abraham, the God of Isaac, and the God of Jacob." Moses hid his face, for he was afraid to look at God.

But God said, "Do not be afraid. I have seen the sadness of my people; I have heard them cry. I know their sufferings, and I have come down to deliver them. I need you to go speak to Pharaoh and tell him to let my people go!"

"Are you kidding? Me? Who am I to talk to Pharaoh?" asked Moses. "Pharaoh kills people right and left! Besides, you know I can barely get words out of my mouth."

"Fine," said God. "Take your brother, Aaron, with you. He's a good speaker, better than you. Be brave. Go! Now!"

Standing in front of Pharaoh's throne, the two brothers did just as God had commanded. "God says this, Pharaoh: 'Let my people go!'"

But the wicked ruler wouldn't listen, and he forced the Israelites to work even harder. Day after day they toiled in the broiling sun; day after day God grieved the abuse.

"I must punish Pharaoh for not listening," God said. "Take your staff, Moses, and hold it over the Nile River. Let him know that I mean business: Let him see the water turn to blood!"

Moses did what God had said. The beautiful river in which his baby basket had been placed turned to blood, just like God said it would. No one could drink the water, and all the fish died. Still, Pharaoh would not listen. Day after day, he brutalized the Israelites.

God was so angry with Pharaoh that he sent eight more warnings. He filled the skies with locusts that blocked the sun and ate the crops. He caused disease to kill the cows and horses and other livestock. He sent thunder and hail that destroyed the crops. Still, nothing. Day after day, Pharaoh's soldiers whipped the people and sent them to bake in the sun.

God was enraged that Pharaoh would not listen. Enough! No more signs. No more warnings.

"Get your people ready, Moses," he said. **"You'll leave this land where you have been treated so badly. Tell all the Israelites they are going on a journey. They won't have enough time to let bread rise and then bake; they will have to make unleavened, flat bread. Tell them to eat a lamb for dinner while standing, ready to go. And tell them to put a little of the blood of the lamb on their doorpost. I am going to move through Egypt, and I will kill the firstborn son of each house that has not been marked."**

God took action that very night. Weeping and wailing filled the streets as the Egyptians, whose doorposts had not been marked with the blood of the lamb, discovered their firstborn sons had been killed.

Then God summoned Moses and Aaron. **"Rise up! It's time to go!"**

Reflection Questions

- There are a lot of brave people in today's story: Moses' mother; Pharaoh's daughter; Miriam; and Moses. What are some of the brave things they do, with God's help? When has God helped you to be brave?

- God speaks to Moses through a burning bush, and God speaks to Pharaoh through the plagues. What are some other ways that God speaks to us?

- God hears the sadness of the people of Israel and comes down to be with them. How is God with you when you are sad?

Moses: Rules to Live By

Based on Exodus 14, 20; Deuteronomy 6

What a horrible night in Egypt! Pharaoh had ignored God for so long, using the Israelites as slaves and refusing to free them, despite many warnings. Almost a dozen times, God had sent Moses to say to Pharaoh, "Let my people go!" God turned the Nile River to blood. God sent locusts, sickened the cattle, and turned the sky black with buzzing gnats.

But Pharaoh would not listen. So God sent a final message: All the firstborn sons of the land would die unless the people were freed. Moses told the Israelites to be ready to flee after they had eaten lamb for dinner and marked their doorposts with blood from those lambs. God promised he would pass over those houses, and no one would die.

Cries of pain and sorrow filled the air when the Egyptian people discovered what God had done. Deciding it was best to have the troublemakers out of his country, Pharaoh relented. "Get out of my sight!" he bellowed. Quickly, as God had instructed, the Israelites left, about a half-million strong.

In those days, there were no cellphones or GPS systems or satellites. There were no computers and no one to rescue you if you were lost. So God led the Israelites with a pillar (or tower) of clouds by day and a pillar of fire by night. They traveled to the shores of the Red Sea, where they camped.

All should have been well, but the peace did not last long. Almost immediately, Pharaoh regretted his decision. *What was I thinking? Who's going to do all the work around here?* Rallying his warriors and lining up 600 of his best chariots, Pharaoh set off to bring back the Israelites.

When the sons and daughters of Israel saw Pharaoh and his army approaching from the desert, they were terrified. Sure that they would be killed, they were scared, and they turned on Moses.

"Were there no graves in Egypt? Did you have to bring us here to bury us? Better to work for the Egyptians than to die in the wilderness!"

"Have no fear!" said Moses. "Stand firm, and you will see how God will save you! He will do the fighting for us."

And God did. That very night, Moses stretched his staff out over the Red Sea, and God parted the waters. The Israelites walked across a dry path, with the waters held back on each side. Safe and sound they went, with Moses holding his staff high, and God protecting them.

Yet onward charged Pharaoh and his armies! His warriors and chariots and horses rushed into the waters. At that very moment, Moses put down his staff. The waters flooded back in, washing over the Egyptian forces until they were destroyed.

Finally, the Israelites were free—and on their way to the Promised Land.

It would take God's people a long time to get to that Promised Land—more than forty years. The people of Israel would wander and wait. They would grumble and complain when things got tough. One time, they even built a golden calf and worshiped it—a terrible thing to do to God!

But, while they wandered, the people also grew incredibly close to God. In the wilderness, God provided the people with manna, special bread from heaven to feed them. In the wilderness, God appeared to Moses in power and glory on Mount Sinai. In the wilderness, God gave the people special rules to live by, rules about how to behave and what to eat and how to worship.

Some of these rules were called the Ten Commandments:

Do not worship any other gods but me.

Do not worship any likeness of me.

Do not misuse my name.

Remember to keep the sabbath holy.

Honor your father and your mother.

You shall not kill.

You shall not commit adultery.

You shall not steal.

You shall not testify falsely against your neighbor.

You shall not covet anything that is your neighbor's.

God gave Moses the Ten Commandments written on special tablets, written by God's own hand. And the people took those tablets and built a special container called an ark to carry them in. This way, they would have the holy words with them always and remember God's presence among them.

God gave the people other beautiful, important rules too.

God said, "Hear, O Israel: The Lord is our God, the Lord alone. You shall love the Lord your God with all your heart, and with all your soul, and with all your might."

God told the people that this rule, this great commandment, was so important that they should say it over and over again to their children and talk about it when they were at home and when they were away, when they lay down and when they got up.

And God also said, "Don't try to get even or hold a grudge. Instead, love your neighbor as you love yourself."

As they journeyed through the wilderness, the people of Israel tried to learn the rules of God. They tried to live in the way God called them to live. Most of the time, they followed the rules. Sadly, sometimes they did not. But God loved them, no matter what.

Finally, after forty years, they came to where the wilderness ended and the Promised Land began. They were filled with questions and excitement as they faced a new future. What would God have in store for them next?

Reflection Questions

- In the story, God asked the Israelites to mark their doors with a special sign, the blood of a lamb, to show that they were faithful to God. What are some other ways that we can show we are faithful to God?

- How do you think the Israelites felt when they left Egypt? When have you felt that way? Have you ever left the place you called home?

- God gave Moses special rules about how to live. Why do you think those rules were so important?

- What are some other rules you know about how we should treat other people? What rules do you know about how we should treat God? Why are those rules important?

Joshua: Leading God's People

Based on Joshua 1-3

For forty years, Moses led the Israelites through the wilderness toward a new place to live. Vowing it would be full of milk and honey, God called it the Promised Land. To former slaves—who never got enough to eat—this new land sounded wonderful. Most important, it would be home.

Within sight of that special land, Moses died. To this day, only God knows where Moses is buried. Israel's new leader, Joshua, faced a huge problem: The land where God was sending the people was already occupied. For hundreds of years, the residents there had fought anyone who tried to move in.

From their camp in the wilderness, the Israelites could see the first city in the Promised Land: Jericho. Fortified with tall and thick walls, the city was packed with strong and beefy people.

"Those walls are huge!" said Joshua, looking down at Jericho. "We need a really good plan if we want to get into the city."

Joshua selected two men to be scouts, to look at the city and figure out a good plan of attack. Joshua sent the men to stay with a woman in Jericho named Rahab, who often had visitors coming and going at odd hours.

"Rahab's house is built right into the city walls," said Joshua, "and there you can get a good view of everything! Figure out the best way to take down the city, for God wants us to have this land."

Most of the people in Jericho did not believe in God. In those days, people usually thought there were many gods and prayed to all of them. God—the real God—wanted people to love and worship only him.

Rahab had heard a great deal about the Israelites and their God. "Your God must be very powerful! He dried up the Red Sea so that you could pass through it and killed those who tried to hurt you! And your people are fearless warriors."

As Rahab was talking to the men, there was a sudden knock at the door. "We know you have spies in there!" a voice called. "Let us in! The king has sent us, demanding that you turn the men over!"

"Quick!" ordered Rahab. "Run up to my roof and hide yourself under the flax that is drying there!" As the Israelites hurried upstairs, hiding themselves under the giant bundles of dried plants called flax, Rahab calmly opened the door.

"Where are those spies?" demanded the king's men. "We know they're here! Turn them over!"

Smoothing back her hair, Rahab shook her head. "I am the only one here," she said. "Those men you seek were here but no longer." And then she pointed to the hills outside the city. "They went that way. If you leave now, you can catch them." The guards raced away, and the Israelites came out of hiding.

"Whew! That was close, Rahab," said the Israelite scouts. "We have to get back to our camp and make our report. Thank you for everything."

"Not so fast!" she said. "I saved your lives. Remember me and my actions."

And they did.

Several weeks later, Joshua gathered the Israelites around Jericho; they were ready to fight.

But God had told Joshua that he had a special plan for Jericho, and it was pretty unusual. The people of Israel wouldn't fight for the city in the regular way, with swords and chariots.

Instead, God told the people, "March around the walls of Jericho for six days and never make a sound. Then, on the seventh day, march around the city seven times. On the seventh time, make as much noise as you can: blowing your trumpets and shouting as loud as you can possibly shout."

The people scratched their heads. It sounded like a crazy idea. How could marching around a city do anything? But that's what God had told Joshua to do, so they agreed to give it a try.

So on day one they went:
March, march, march, march, march.
And they never made a sound.

And on day two:
March, march, march, march, march.
And they never made a sound.

And on day three:
March, march, march, march, march.
And they never made a sound.

And on day four:
March, march, march, march, march.
And they never made a sound.

And on day five:
March, march, march, march, march.
And they never made a sound.

And on day six:
March, march, march, march, march.
And they never made a sound.

And then, on day seven:
March, march, march, march, march.
But this time, they did make a sound. They blew their trumpets and sounded their horns and shouted at the top of their voices. And when they did…the walls came tumbling down!

After the walls fell, the Israelites destroyed every living thing inside the city—except for Rahab and her family, who joined the Israelite people as they settled in Jericho.

Joshua led the people in many other battles, though most of them involved swords and fighting, not just marching around walls. When they conquered a city, the Israelites got rid of the kings and leaders who didn't believe in the one, true God and selected leaders who did believe in God. Slowly the people of God spread through the land, growing their families, building homes, and starting new lives.

Finally, after lots of wandering and waiting and sadness, the people of Israel were living in the land that God had promised them. But they were not alone in the land; they lived as a people in the midst of other peoples. Even in the Promised Land, the people had to learn to follow and trust in God alone.

Reflection Questions

- Rahab was not a leader or teacher. She was not a princess or a judge. She was not someone that you would expect to be important. But her actions helped God and God's people. Who are some people in your life that help God and God's people, even when it's not expected?

- How do you think the people of Israel felt marching around the city without making a sound? Is that usually how people invade a city? Why do you think God might have asked them to do it this way instead?

- On the last day, God told the people to sing and shout and make lots of noise. Have you ever wanted to sing and shout and make lots of noise to God? Why? What do you think it would be like to do that in church?

After the days of Moses and Joshua, Israel needed other leaders to guide Israel. So God raised up judges. These were not black-robed judges like we have today in courtrooms but judges who interpreted God's law, fought on the battlefields, and inspired others to stand up for God. Most were deep and thoughtful. One was wild and crazy-eyed. All were brave and risked their own lives to protect God's people.

One by one, the judges led, keeping order in Israel and trying to remind the people to remain faithful to God. One of those judges was Deborah.

Sitting under a beautiful palm tree in her yard, Deborah listened to people who were angry with each other; it was her job to make decisions for people when they could not agree. Whatever she decided was law.

One day, Deborah heard news that made her stomach sink like a stone. Philistines—longtime enemies of the Israelites—were raging through the countryside, killing the men and kidnapping the women and children. Outraged, Deborah summoned the leader of Israel's army, Barak.

"Our God commands you to go out and fight the Philistines and their leader, Sisera. Leave now!"

But Barak would not go to war without Deborah; she gave him strength and confidence.

"Surely I will go with you," Deborah said. "And another woman will be needed to complete the battle as well."

Together, Deborah and Barak rode out on horseback, leading 10,000 men to the top of Mount Tabor, where they could see for miles. Each day, more and more Philistines, along with their strong chariots and fierce weapons, arrived. The Israelites were outnumbered, and the Philistines had better weapons. Everyone became afraid.

But Deborah trusted God to lead them, and she prayed and listened for God's instructions. At the right moment, she said to Barak, "God says that now is the time! Today is the day that God will deliver Sisera into your hands!"

Surging down Mount Tabor with their soldiers, Barak and Deborah could see fierce anger and hatred on the faces of the Philistines. What chance did the Israelites have?

But God was on their side. At that moment, the sky broke open with thunderous claps of lightning. Pouring down with unprecedented force, rain flooded the hillside below, trapping the Philistines in a sea of mud. All of the army, except Sisera, the general, fell to Israelite swords.

Like a scared dog, Sisera ran away and hid in the tent of a woman named Jael. "Give me some milk!" he said. "I'm exhausted!"

Jael gave him milk. Then, when he was asleep, she also gave him a tent peg to the head, killing him. Deborah's prophecy had been right. For a time, Israel was safe.

Other judges rose to protect and lead the people of Israel. Sadly, the Philistines, although defeated in battle by Deborah and Barak and other judges, also grew in numbers and strength.

But God continued to work his wonders. Years after Deborah led Israel, a boy named Samson was born. God told Samson's parents to raise him as a Nazirite, a holy man, and God gave him great strength. God told Samson's mother never to cut his hair, or he would lose his power. A bit of a wild child, Samson saw his strength and bravery increase each year, until he too stepped into that mighty line of judges.

Some people were scared by Samson's deeds. The Bible tells of a time that he tied 300 foxes together by their tails and lit a fire under them to scare the Philistines. Once he singlehandedly killed 1,000 Philistines using only the jawbone of a donkey. Those were terribly bloody days in Israel.

One day the Philistines sent a woman named Delilah to trap Samson.

"Find out what makes him so strong!" said the Philistines to Delilah. "And then we'll know how to destroy him."

Sitting close to Samson, Delilah asked: "What makes you so strong? How might you be bound so that one could subdue you?"

A great riddle-teller, Samson answered: "If my enemies bind me with seven fresh bowstrings, then I shall become weak." While the Philistines waited in an inner chamber, Delilah bound Samson with fresh bowstrings.

"The Philistines are upon you, Samson!" she said. And the Philistines rushed in to capture the strong man—but he snapped the bowstrings like they were matchsticks.

"You have mocked me, Samson!" said Delilah. "Tell me how you might be bound."

"If you tie me up with new ropes that have never been used, I will become weak, like any other man," answered Samson.

Out came the ropes. In rushed the Philistines. And the game went on, riddle after riddle. Again and again, Delilah asked Samson how he could be defeated. And again and again, Samson tricked Delilah with fake answers.

One day, Delilah appealed to Samson's heart. "How can you say, 'I love you,' when your heart is not with me? You have made fun of me without stopping," whined Delilah.

Finally Samson gave in and told the truth. "A razor has never touched my head," he admitted. "If my hair is cut, I will be like any other man."

That very day, Delilah cut Samson's hair while he was sleeping. When he woke up, his strength was gone—and the Philistines captured him! Gouging out his eyes, they blinded him, tied him up, and carried him off to jail.

For weeks, Samson waited, praying and thinking. Then one day he was brought from jail so the Philistines could make fun of him. Propped up against two strong pillars, Samson was surrounded by more than 3,000 people.

"Big, strong man!" they jeered. "Where's your strength now? You look like nothing more than a feather, so light you could be blown away!"

While he was in jail, Samson's hair had grown and some of his strength had returned. So Samson called to God. "Remember me, I pray you. Strengthen me only this once, O God, that I may have revenge upon our enemies." And grasping the two pillars, Samson pushed with all his might, causing the entire building to fall down and crush the Philistines. In his final act, Samson killed more people than he had killed in his lifetime.

And, for a time, Israel was safe once again. But the people of Israel were wandering further and further away from God. They were not following the laws that God had given them, and they were not listening to God's judges that he had sent to lead them. Perhaps the time had come for the people to have a king.

Reflection Questions

- Judges were leaders whom God called to guide Israel. What qualities do you think would make a good judge?

- Samson was a judge, even though he made some big mistakes. What can this tell us about the people God chooses?

- Where did the judges of Israel get their power?

Hannah & Samuel: Keeping Promises

Based on 1 Samuel 1-4

Sometimes, just when we think tears and sadness might last forever, God acts—and wonderful things happen. About 3,500 years ago, that's the way it was for a young woman named Hannah. God transformed her tears into joy. God gave Hannah what she wanted most—and it just so happened that her gift from God became Israel's great joy as well.

Early one morning, Hannah stood and cried at the temple in Shiloh. Pouring out her heart, she asked God for her deepest desire: a son. Month after month, she and her husband, Elkanah, tried to make a baby. But year after year went by, and Hannah did not become pregnant. Her arms ached with emptiness.

"Please, O God, please give me a son," Hannah prayed. "If you give me my heart's deepest desire—a son—I will give him back to you to serve in your temple."

Hannah was praying so hard that the priest thought she must be drunk—her lips were moving and yet no sound came out.

"What is the matter with you?" asked Eli, the priest. "Why do you just stand there, with your mouth moving? How long will you make a drunken spectacle of yourself?!"

"Oh, no, sir! Please understand that I am a woman sorely troubled, and I am deep in prayer! I have been pouring out my soul before God."

With those words, Eli knew that Hannah's words and thoughts were sincere. "Go in peace," he said, "and may the God of Israel grant the request you have made of him."

Shortly after that, Hannah found that her prayer had been answered. She gave birth to a son and named him Samuel, which means, "God has heard."

Hannah loved the quiet moments she had with her boy. But she also remembered her promise to God. When Samuel was about three years old, Hannah took him back to the temple at Shiloh. Brushing her hand over his little head, she handed her beloved son to Eli, the same priest who had thought she was drunk.

She said to Eli, "I am that woman who stood before you. For this child I prayed, and the Lord has granted me the prayer I made to him. And now I am keeping my vow—that I would lend him to the Lord, in whose service is perfect freedom."

And so it was that Samuel grew up at the temple, learning scripture, history, and worship life. But Samuel and his mother stayed close. Each year Hannah would knit Samuel a woolen coat and bring it to him so that he would stay warm and dry.

The temple at Shiloh was a wonderful place. It housed the most important symbol to the Israelite people: the Ark of the Covenant of God. Within the Ark was the great symbol of God's law and love, the two stone tablets of the Ten Commandments.

But there was also trouble at the temple. Eli had two sons who were mean and did a lot of bad things, including not taking good care of the Ark. They even lost the Ark in a battle to the Philistines.

One night as Samuel lay sleeping, he was awakened by a voice calling, "Samuel, Samuel!"

The boy got up and ran to Eli, saying, "Here I am, for you called me!" But the old priest said, "I did not call you. Go lie down again." So Samuel went back to bed.

But once again, as Samuel lay sleeping, he was awakened by a voice calling, "Samuel, Samuel!"

Again, the boy got up and ran to Eli, saying, "Here I am, for you called me!"

"But I did not call you," said the old priest. "Go lie down again." Once more Samuel went back to bed.

Then the voice came a third time, calling, "Samuel!" Samuel!" And Samuel ran to Eli. This time, the old priest understood that it was God calling Samuel. "Go lie down again," said Eli. "And if the voice calls again, say, 'Speak, Lord, for your servant is listening.'" And that is what Samuel did.

God spoke to Samuel, saying, "Behold, I am about to do something in Israel that will make both ears of anyone who hears of it tingle! I am going to destroy the house of Eli, because his sons curse me and lie about me. I have told him that I would punish them, and the time is coming close."

Do I tell Eli this hard message? thought Samuel. He loved his teacher and priest.

Eli asked the boy. **"What is it that God told you? Don't hide anything from me."** So Samuel told him the truth, keeping nothing back. And Eli said: **"It is the Lord; let him do what seems good to him."**

In the end, God punished the house of Eli, and none of Eli's sons became rulers in Israel. Samuel, who was faithful to God and the lessons Eli taught him, grew up to become a great judge in Israel—and the last one.

Samuel stood at a crossroads of history. The time of the great judges was ending, and Israel was asking for a king.

Faithful Samuel continued to listen to God's voice, letting go of his role as judge and instead serving as prophet for God and anointing the first king of Israel. The days ahead would not be easy, but important things rarely are.

Reflection Questions

- Hannah wanted a child desperately and prayed to God with all her might. Have you ever prayed like that? What was it like? How did God answer?

- Samuel's mother and her faithfulness led Samuel to serve God. What have your parents taught you, by word and example, about loving and serving God?

- When God called to Samuel, Samuel thought it was Eli calling him. Have you ever heard God calling you? What did God's voice sound like?

- Sometimes circumstances get hard, but it is often at those times that we find our strength. When have you faced a hard situation and learned from it?

Samuel: Pointing the Way for Israel

Based on 1 Samuel 9, 16

Ever since he heard God calling him as a little boy, Samuel, the last great judge of Israel, walked closely with God. And now, as God's people kept demanding a king, Samuel did two things: He listened to the people, and he sought God's voice.

"Find us a king," the people said, "so that we can fight off those pesky Philistines! They keep gouging out our eyes and stealing our children."

"You don't need a king!" said Samuel. "God is our king, and that is enough."

But the people would not back down. "We must have a king! We need to be like other nations! We need a king who will lead us to victory in war!"

When Samuel brought their demands to God, he heard a different side of the story.

"Tell them what a king would do," God said to Samuel. "Tell them that a king will send their sons to war and will send their daughters away as common workers. A king will take the best of their vineyards and their cattle. A king will take away their livelihoods and rob them of their freedom."

But the people would not give up. They kept chipping away at Samuel. Over and over, they repeated their call: They needed a king.

Finally, God relented. "They will have their king," God said. "But they will not choose their own leader. I will provide one."

God chose a young man named Saul to be the first king of Israel. That very day, Saul was out searching for several donkeys that had wandered off from his father's land. Saul came to Samuel's town, looking for his donkeys, and God told Samuel that Saul was the king he had chosen.

"Sir, I am looking for my donkeys. Can you help me?" said Saul to Samuel.

"Give no further thought to your donkeys," said Samuel. "They have found their way home to your father, and God has other things in mind for you!"

With those words, Samuel produced a vial of very special oil. Pouring the oil over Saul's head, he anointed him, saying: "The Lord has appointed you ruler over his people. You will save them from their enemies."

"But I am just a shepherd," Saul protested, "from the least of the tribes of Israel!"

"God has called you," said Samuel. "Your call is a holy one, and God will be with you."

Saul wasn't at all sure he wanted to be king. In fact, he ran away and hid in a big pile of luggage! But the people searched for Saul and found him, carrying him out while shouting, "Long live the king!" Like it or not, Saul became king over Israel.

Israel finally had the king it had wanted for so long. But Saul did not turn out to be the right kind of king. An anxious man, full of worries, Saul made decisions on his own instead of waiting for God. And sometimes, when God gave him specific orders, Saul did not follow them as closely as God wanted.

So, unbeknownst to Saul, God told Samuel that it was time for Israel to have a new king: one who would lead with brains and heart and soul—one who would do exactly as God said. Samuel was greatly troubled by the news, for he had grown fond of Saul.

"How long will you grieve his loss?" asked God. "Fill your jar with oil and set out. Go to the family of Jesse, near Bethlehem, for I have found Israel's next king among his sons." So Samuel did as God had asked and went to the family of Jesse.

When Samuel saw the oldest son of Jesse, a fine-looking boy, he was excited. Surely this is the Lord's anointed, he thought. He is tall and brave and handsome and smart.

But the Lord whispered to Samuel: "This is not the one. I see human beings differently than you do. You cannot see into a man's soul like I can."

One by one, Jesse brought seven of his sons before Samuel, in order of age. One by one, God rejected them.

"Jesse, are all your sons here?" asked Samuel. "All except the youngest," said Jesse. "He is out tending the sheep, while the rest of us are doing important work here."

"Send for him!" said Samuel. "Bring him here. We will not sit down until we see him."

And David, Jesse's youngest son, was brought before Samuel. Tall, handsome, and ruddy-cheeked, he had beautiful eyes.

"This is the one!" said God to Samuel. "Anoint him, for this is the next king of Israel!"

So Samuel took his vial and poured the oil over David's head. God's Spirit came upon David mightily on that day. But because Saul was still on the throne, David went back to his sheep, until the time was right.

In the wilderness, the hours are long, and a shepherd must always be on guard. Sometimes David had to kill lions and bears in order to protect his sheep. Yet the life of a shepherd is also full of solitude and quiet. Under the stars and alone in the sun, David grew into both a poet and a musician, praising God in music and song.

And it was his musical abilities that led David to Saul. Full of his old fears, King Saul was soothed by one thing: music. The call went out for a musician to work in the court—to bring joy and peace to the old king—and David soon joined Saul's company. Becoming best friends with Saul's son, Jonathan, David carried Saul's armor in battle, played his lyre, and became like a second son to the old king.

Peace came to Saul's heart—but only for a little while.

Reflection Questions

- The people of Israel wanted a king, even though it wasn't good for them. When have you wanted something that wasn't good for you?

- God looks at people differently from the way we do; we look at the outside, but God looks at the heart. What do you think God is looking for in our hearts? What might he find?

- What helps you trust in God when you are afraid?

- Music helped David praise God, and it helped Saul feel less scared. How do you feel when you listen to music? What music makes you feel close to God?

Although David had been anointed by Samuel to lead Israel as king, he didn't take the crown for several years. David spent his time as a shepherd, protecting his sheep from wild animals, and as a musician, writing beautiful songs to praise God.

David's brothers were off fighting the Philistines, and Jesse, their father, grew lonely for them. In those days, there were no newspapers, computers, or telephones, so news was limited. Jesse called David in from the fields and told him to find his brothers.

"Take them some food, and find out what's going on," Jesse told David. "I hear horrible things about a giant warrior, and I want to know my boys are still alive."

So David packed his bags with cheese and bread and wine and set out in search of his brothers. When he found the battlefield on which they were supposedly fighting, it was quiet. Finally, David located his brothers behind a set of high rocks.

For forty days straight, the Israelites had been taunted by a giant named Goliath. Goliath was nine feet tall, more than three feet taller than the average man. His armor was so heavy that he clanked when he walked, and his biceps were so big they looked like cannon balls. Every morning Goliath would appear from over the hill, heckling the Israelites.

"Send just one man out," Goliath said. "I will fight him. If I lose, we will be your slaves. But if he loses—and he WILL lose—you will bow down before us forever!

"I'll fight him!" David vowed. "I'll take him down!"

His brothers howled. "Get outta here," said one.

"We're men! You're a boy. And boys stay home!" growled another.

David thought of how the Israelites had been slaves in Egypt and how Moses had led them across the Red Sea. He thought of the forty years they had spent wandering in the wilderness, waiting for God to lead them to the Promised Land. David knew they must stay strong and not lose their freedom—or everything they had been given, everything for which they had fought so hard, would be lost.

Each morning, Goliath mocked the Israelites. "You're like little birds, ready to fly away!! Is there no one willing to stand up to me? You're all COWARDS!"

David grew angrier by the day. "Who does he think he is?! He is making fun of God's army!"

David ached to hit the giant with a rock or two from his slingshot. But he knew he couldn't storm out onto the field as a rogue soldier. Throwing back his shoulders and taking a deep breath, David marched to King Saul.

"Let me fight Goliath," said David. "I will kill him with my slingshot."

"You're just a boy!" said Saul. "Our lives are at stake here."

"I've killed bears and lions with my bare hands when they came after my sheep," said David. "I promise you this: I will not miss."

Saul looked one more time at the handsome boy. Then, quietly nodding his head, Saul held out a suit of armor. David put it on, but it was much too heavy. Once he was out of Saul's sight, David quickly stripped off the heavy metal suit. Kneeling down by a stream, he selected five smooth stones and loaded his slingshot with the first stone.

"Help me, Lord," David prayed. "Fill me with your strength and help me to protect your people."

Like a strong young colt, David walked onto the battlefield. Once more, Goliath ridiculed him.

"They sent YOU?" Goliath laughed. "They sent a boy to do a MAN'S job?"

David had had enough—and so had Israel. With a smooth flick of his wrist, David propelled a rock right into the middle of Goliath's forehead. The giant was dead. To make sure, David cut off his head. In stunned silence, the Philistines ran for their lives.

David's strength and confidence in battle would lead the Israelites to victory against the Philistines, over and over again.

But it was not time for that yet. For now, Saul was still the king of Israel. So, after his great victory over Goliath, David returned to the life that he knew: the life of a shepherd out in the fields.

As David came near to his father's flock, the sheep welcomed him back without a second thought: He was their shepherd. Once again, David watched over them, cared for them, led them, and protected them.

At night, when the sheep were safely gathered together, David would pull out his harp and write prayers and songs of praise to God. David's songs were about the things that he knew: sheep and water and fields and God's unrelenting love. David's voice combined with the notes of his harp to make the most beautiful music. The music would drift through the air, soothing the sheep and rising up to God like smoke from a fire.

David sang,

"The Lord is my shepherd,
I shall not be in want.
He makes me lie down in green pastures,
And leads me beside still waters.
He revives my soul
And guides me along right pathways for his Name's sake.
Though I walk through the valley of the shadow of death,
I shall fear no evil;
For you are with me,
Your rod and your staff, they comfort me.
You spread a table before me in the presence of those who trouble me;
You have anointed my head with oil,
And my cup is running over.
Surely your goodness and mercy shall follow me all the days of my life,
And I will dwell in the house of the Lord for ever."

This song would become one of the most beloved verses in the Bible—Psalm 23. And David, inspired by God, wrote from his heart and from what he knew as a faithful shepherd.

Years later, after Saul died on the battlefield, David rose to be the greatest king of Israel. God was within him and behind him, supporting and guiding him at every turn. David had learned to be king in the most unlikely place: out in the open fields, surrounded by sheep.

About 1,000 years later, in the same town where David was born, another shepherd is born: Jesus. Like David protecting those in his care, Jesus is our protector. Like David playing the harp for King Saul, Jesus is music to our souls. He is always next to us, walking beside us and keeping us strong. As David was ready to lay down his life to save his people, Jesus died so that we might live. We are forever safe in God's embrace because Jesus carries us night and day, even when we can't see him.

Reflection Questions

- David learned to be a king by being a shepherd. How is being a shepherd like being a king? How is it different?

- Why do you think David fought Goliath with his slingshot instead of a sword and without wearing any armor? What might we learn from this?

- Have you ever faced a problem that seemed really big or a bully who tried to make you feel small and powerless? How did you handle that situation? What can you learn from David about how to deal with situations that seem impossible?

Psalm 23 is from The Book of Common Prayer.

Solomon: Fit for a King

Based on 1 Kings 3:1-28

King David lived a long and worthy life, uniting all of the tribes of Israel and praising God in word and song. A brave warrior and eloquent man, David loved God dearly.

When David died, his son, Solomon, became the king of Israel. Solomon was a humble man and a deep thinker. One day, God appeared to Solomon in a dream and told him he could have whatever he asked for. Sometimes kings and queens want money and power. But not Solomon. Solomon asked God for one thing: wisdom. God was pleased with Solomon's request and gave him what he asked for, making Solomon so wise that kings and queens from other countries would travel to Solomon's court to hear his great words.

One day, two poor women arrived at the palace, passionately arguing their case in front of King Solomon. They lived in the same house, and both had given birth to baby boys within a few days of each other. One of the babies had died—and the women were arguing about who should raise the remaining baby.

"She killed my son!" said the first woman. "I gave birth first, and then three days later this woman gave birth. We were together in the house—there was no one else there. Her son died because she rolled over in bed and laid on him! Then she got up and took MY baby while I was in bed, asleep, with him at my breast."

"No!" said the second woman. "That's not the way it happened at all! You're lying!"

"She put her dead son in bed with me," said the first woman. "Right away, when I woke up and saw the dead baby next to me, I knew it wasn't my son!"

"You're lying!" yelled the second woman. And so they argued before King Solomon, back and forth, back and forth.

What would you do if you were the king? How would solve the problem? Who should get the baby? Should one woman get the baby? If so, which one?

"I have a solution," said Solomon. "Guards, bring me a sword, and divide the living boy in two! Give half to one woman, and half to the other."

Gasps echoed throughout the room as the guard raised his sword for the terrible deed.

"Do not kill him!" screamed the first woman. "Give her the boy!"

"It shall be neither mine nor yours," said the second woman. "Divide it!"

In that moment, Solomon knew who the real mother was—a real mother would never allow her child to be put to death. Even if it meant that she would never see her son again, a real mother would do all she could to guarantee her child's safety. Wise King Solomon had never planned to cut the baby in half; he was using that threat as a test.

"Give the boy to its mother," said Solomon, "now that we know who the real mother is!"

This was just the beginning of Solomon's wisdom. Solomon said many wise things when he was king. Some of his words of wisdom were written down in Proverbs and other books of the Bible, so that people could read them and remember them for hundreds of years to come. Things like:

"Don't ever stop being kind and truthful.
   Let kindness and truth show in all you do."

"A gentle answer will calm a person's anger.
   But an unkind answer will cause more anger."

"A friend loves you all the time.
   A brother is always there to help you."

"A foolish person loses his temper.
   But a wise person controls his anger."

"Do what is right and fair.
   That is more important to the Lord than animal sacrifices."

The wisest thing that Solomon did was to build a beautiful temple in Jerusalem where all believers could worship God. One day Solomon realized that he was living in a huge palace, but God didn't have a place to call home. The Ark of the Covenant, the holy container that the people of God had built to carry the tablets of the law that God gave to Moses, was just sitting outside in a tent! Solomon knew that God deserved better.

So Solomon gathered the greatest craftsmen that he could find: people who were skilled weavers crafted complicated tapestries and curtains; woodworkers carved beautiful angels from olive wood; jewelers made intricate lampstands and incense bowls; and stonemasons carved an enormous altar, on which the priests would place the offerings to God. They all gave their very best to decorate

God's house, because they knew that God had given them everything, and they wanted to give back in praise and worship of God.

It took Solomon and the people seven years to build the temple, God's special house of worship. And when it was finished, they had a huge celebration, a festival of dedication. The priests carried the Ark of the Covenant into the temple, to a special place called the Holy of Holies. And as the priests carried the ark, the people prayed and cried out with joy and gave offerings to God, so many offerings that you couldn't even count them all.

As the Ark settled in the temple, a cloud covered it, and the glory of the Lord filled the house of the Lord, just as a cloud of God's glory had covered Mount Sinai when Moses received the tablets of the law.

Solomon, that wise king, fell on his knees in front of all the people. Can you imagine? A king, falling on his knees? But Solomon was wise, and he knew that everyone, even kings, fall down before God, the King of kings and Lord of lords. So Solomon knelt down and lifted his hands to heaven and prayed to God, saying, **"Blessed be the Lord, the God of Israel, who has kept all of his promises. There is no God like you, in heaven above or on the earth beneath. Therefore devote yourselves to God alone!"**

For the next forty years, Solomon used his deep wisdom to resolve complicated questions for the people of Israel. As king, Solomon did his best to lead people in worshiping and following God. Still, Solomon was only human and he made mistakes—some big and some small. He didn't follow God perfectly. God knew that the people needed a real king, one who would not fail.

It would be a long time before the real king would come, born in a manger in Bethlehem. But that's a story for another day.

Reflection Questions

- Solomon is a king who is known for his wisdom. Do you know anyone who is very wise? What kind of things does that person do or say?

- Solomon can ask God for anything that he wants, and he asks God for wisdom. If you could ask God for anything you wanted, what would you ask for? What do think God would say about your choice?

- Solomon was famous for writing the Proverbs—wise statements about life and the world. Which is your favorite? What other statements of wisdom are important to you?

- Solomon built the temple for the Lord. What does today's story tell us about that temple? If you were building a temple for God today, what would it look like?

When King Solomon died, dark times came over Israel. Over the next several hundred years, Israel was ruled by kings and queens, some who were good, and others who were bad. Two particularly evil rulers were a married couple, King Ahab and Queen Jezebel. Whenever any voice rose up in the kingdom to praise God, they would stamp it out. As the nation groaned under their ways, the kingdom—which had been united under David and Solomon—crumbled.

Without good rulers guiding the country, God had to find another way to reach his people—and did so through special messengers called prophets. One of those prophets was named Elijah.

Like most Israelites, Elijah was starving—for whenever there is much conflict and war, there is also much hunger. "Go to a town called Zarephath (ZEHR-uh-fath)," said God to Elijah. "There, a woman will feed you."

If I can't find this woman, I will die, thought Elijah. *But I'm so hungry that maybe it will be better that way.* Stumbling into Zarephath, Elijah was famished and thirsty. Then he saw a tired old woman, bending and stooping, bending and stooping. *Could that be bread in her hand? She's holding something!!*

"Give me that bread!" said Elijah. "If I eat, I might last another day."

"I have no bread, sir!" answered the woman. "I am collecting sticks to build a fire for my son! All I can do is make us a few biscuits. We may starve to death soon."

"Do not be afraid," said Elijah. "Keep finding the sticks you need. But when you've cooked some biscuits, bring me a handful first. If you do so, God says your oil jugs will overflow, and your flour bins will always be full."

Shaking her head, the woman stared at Elijah as though he were a talking goat. Still, several hours later she brought him warm bread. For the first time in months, Elijah's stomach was full. And just as Elijah had promised, the woman's oil jug never ran out, and she had plenty of flour—enough to make food for herself and her son in the days and weeks to come. Slowly, the boy gained back his strength.

Onlookers might have thought Elijah was selfish, asking a hungry mother to feed him before giving food to her starving son. But Elijah was sending a message: Put God first, and everything else will fall into place.

That was a message that Queen Jezebel and King Ahab did not want to hear. With hearts as cold as an Arctic winter, they went after those who loved God. They demanded that their subjects praise their god, called Ba'al, and they hired 450 false prophets to worship their god.

"Ba'al is all-powerful," they jeered. "With just the tiniest snap of his all-powerful fingers, he can make the heavens open and the rains pour forth!"

Really? Thought Elijah. *Have you come out of your palace and looked around lately? Nothing is growing: not grass, not flowers, not even weeds.* At first Elijah did not voice his opinion because he was listening hard for God's clear directions. But finally, he heard God's voice.

"The Lord has spoken!" Elijah told King Ahab. "Assemble all the people at Mount Carmel, especially your prophets who sing and praise Ba'al."

"Fine," said King Ahab. "Settling this conflict between me and your God will be the most fun I've had in a long time."

When the day came, Elijah stood strong. "I am just one lone voice," he said. "But I speak on behalf of God, the one God, living and true. There is no greater power."

Surrounded by the evil prophets, Elijah told them to gather around their altar. "Call on Ba'al to light a fire," he said. "Ask him to set fire to the altar. And I will call my God, the real God, to do the same."

All morning long, the prophets of God danced around their altar. "Answer us, mighty Ba'al, answer us!" As the hours dragged on, they began to limp. They became so tired that they were bent over, and their arms dragged on the ground.

At noon Elijah mocked them, saying: "Maybe your god is meditating! Maybe he has wandered away on a journey! Or maybe he has fallen asleep and needs to be awakened!" As the shadows lengthened, Elijah called out to the people of Israel, saying: "Come closer to me!" Elijah dug a trench around the altar and filled it with water. Then he dumped water on the altar three times, until it was completely soaked. Surely, the people thought, no fire could consume an altar that was under water.

Elijah prayed. "Show yourself, O Lord of all. Let it be known this day in Israel that I am your servant and that I have done all this at your bidding. Help everyone to know that you are God and that you have turned the hearts of your people back to you."

Fire suddenly burst from the sky. Everything—including wood, stones, dust, and even the water around the altar—was consumed. When the people saw what had happened, they fell on their faces and said: "The Lord is indeed God; the Lord is indeed God!" But two people remained standing: Jezebel and Ahab.

"Seize the prophets of Ba'al," proclaimed Elijah. "Do not let one escape!" And the evil prophets were put to death.

Jezebel was enraged by Elijah's actions, and she put out word that he must be destroyed. But Elijah escaped into the wilderness, where he wandered for forty days and nights. An angel brought him food and water, and Elijah searched for God. Elijah stood looking into the face of an earthquake, searching for God. He looked into a fire, searching for God. And he stood in the wind, waiting...waiting to hear from God.

But God was not in the earthquake. Nor was God in the fire or the wind. Finally, in silence, Elijah heard a still, small voice.

"What are you doing here, Elijah?" asked God.

"My enemies are seeking to kill me," said Elijah. "Give me direction."

And so God did, filling his days and nights with tasks that only Elijah could perform. When Elijah was a very old man, he had an experience unlike any other person in the Bible: He was taken up into heaven in a great chariot of fire, led by horses of fire, fitting for one who had called fire down from heaven to help God's people believe.

God also sent other prophets: Isaiah and Jeremiah and Micah. They, like Elijah, asked people to be faithful to God alone, to turn their hearts to God and live lives that proclaimed God. But the people didn't listen to Elijah and the others. They turned away from God and started worshiping other gods. They stopped living according to the rules that God had given them through Moses. God loved his people so much, but their bad actions had consequences. Soon the people of Israel were captured by other armies. Their holy temple was destroyed, and they were sent away to faraway lands. They had wandered far from God, and now they were far from home as well. But God continued to be with them, loving them and calling to them, even in their darkest moments.

Reflection Questions

- Why is it important to put God first in our lives? What are some ways that we can try to put God first?

- Elijah heard from God in the silence. Why is silence important when listening for God's voice?

- Two times in Elijah's story, he is hungry and other people bring him bread and water. Who are the people that feed Elijah? Why is that important? What other stories of special bread have we heard this year? When do we eat special bread together?

Prophets in Exile:
Daniel and the Lions' Den

Based on Daniel 1, 2, 3, and 6

magine if you were a Jewish refugee, forced to live in a foreign land, a place that worshiped foreign gods. How would you keep your faith strong? Your beloved temple in Jerusalem had been demolished. There were no Bibles in homes; there was no way to keep in touch with friends and fellow believers.

Such was the case for Daniel, a refugee from Judah, the southern part of Israel. Captured as a boy and taken into exile by the Babylonians, Daniel had grown up in the court of Nebuchadnezzar (Neb-uh-kuhd-NEZ-er), the Babylonian king. Much like Moses growing up in Pharaoh's court, Daniel was educated in the language and ways of his captors—yet he never forgot his roots.

Some people would have gone completely over to the other side, forgetting their own faith. But not Daniel and his three friends: Shadrach, Meshach, and Abednego (SHAD-rak, MEE-shak, and Uh-BED-ni-goh). They prayed together, followed God's food laws, kept in top physical shape, and quietly held onto their faith.

Nebuchadnezzar was so impressed with Daniel over the years that he appointed him ruler over the whole province of Babylon. And Daniel appointed his boyhood friends to help him rule. Little did the king know that Daniel would grow to be one of Israel's most visionary prophets, giving strength and comfort to people, even thousands of years after he died.

One day Nebuchadnezzar ordered that a golden statue be made in his image, and he told everyone to bow down before it every time they heard the sound of music in the streets.

"No exceptions!" he cried out. "Every time you hear those happy sounds of pipe, lyre, or harp, you will bow down to my image!"

Shadrach, Meshach, and Abednego refused. (No doubt Daniel refused as well, but he was off in another part of the country.) Enraged, Nebuchadnezzar had the men brought before him. "I've treated you so well! All you have to do is bow before my statue, and everything will be fine!"

"But you are not God!" they replied. "We only bow and pray before the God of Israel, the God of the universe. After all, that is the first commandment that God gave us!"

"If you do not worship me," the king snarled, "I will have you thrown into a fiery furnace, and there you will die!"

"God is our only defense," replied the three friends. "We will not worship you, and we will not worship your gods."

Filled with rage, Nebuchadnezzar's face became distorted. "As you wish!" he screamed. "Heat up that furnace seven times hotter than normal!"

Tied up like Thanksgiving turkeys, the men were thrown into the white-hot, blazing furnace. But as the flames grew higher, the king and people saw an unbelievable sight: Shadrach, Meshach, and Abednego walked around in the furnace! They were unharmed, accompanied by a fourth figure.

"How can they still be alive?" said the king. "And we threw three men into the furnace, not four." And then he understood. The fourth figure was God—walking with the three young men, protecting them in the midst of the raging fire. In that moment, the king's heart was softened and his eyes opened. He joined forces with God.

"There is no other god who is able to deliver in this way!" said the king. "Shadrach, Meshach, and Abednego, servants of the Most High God, come out! From now on, anyone who speaks badly of the God of Israel will be torn limb from limb!"

Years passed. Daniel continued to love God and served the Babylonians as a top government official. After Nebuchadnezzar's death, a new king, Darius, rose to power. He did not love God but thought highly of Daniel.

Daniel is such a bright man and a hard worker, he thought. *I'll promote him to run the country. I can really use his skills. He will report only to me.* But some people were jealous of Daniel and did not want him to succeed. Behind closed doors, they hatched a plan to get rid of Daniel. They knew he went home to his bedroom three times a day, knelt down, faced toward Jerusalem, and prayed. Cautiously—and catching Darius when he was preoccupied with kingly matters—they stood before him.

"O king," they said. "No one should pledge allegiance to anyone—human or divine—but you. We suggest you throw anyone who prays to their God into the lions' den for dinner. Here, sign this!" And they thrust a document into Darius's hands.

Without thinking of the damage it might cause, Darius signed the decree. Even though Daniel knew the deadly order had been signed, he stayed true to his faith. As he had done for years, Daniel walked home to pray three times a day, pouring out his heart to God, whom he had loved his whole life.

As those with evil intentions do, the conspirators hid themselves, nodding and winking, waiting in secret. Flinging open Daniel's bedroom door one bright morning, they found him on his knees.

"You have to kill Daniel," they screamed to Darius. "You signed that decree, and it cannot be broken!"

Sadly, the king nodded, for even kings have to keep the vows they make. Daniel was thrown into the lions' den, and the gate was locked with Darius's own seal. But that night, sleep eluded the king, and he fasted—he didn't eat a thing. When he hurried to the lions' den the next morning, he found Daniel still there but very much alive!

"O Daniel," said Darius, "servant of the living God, has your God been able to deliver you from the lions?

"O king, live forever!" Daniel replied. "My God sent his angel and shut the lions' mouths so they would not hurt me. I was found blameless before him, and also before you, O king. I have done no wrong."

Overjoyed, Darius commanded that Daniel be restored as high ruler of Babylon, subject only to him.

And the bad men who arranged for Daniel to be eaten by the lions? The king snapped his fingers— and the lions went to bed with very full stomachs that night.

Daniel and his three friends remained faithful to God, even in a foreign land, even when it was hard. Their faithfulness set an example for many, teaching other Israelites how to be faithful and bringing people to know, love, and serve the one true God! Although they were far from home, God continued to be with the Israelites. God loved them so much that one day soon, God would send leaders to bring them back to their special city, Jerusalem, so that they could rebuild and worship God in the temple once more.

Reflection Questions

- Daniel always put God first. How do you put God first in your life?

- Daniel prayed on his knees, facing Jerusalem. Where and how do you pray?

- God was with the three men in the furnace and with Daniel in the lions' den. How is God with you in scary times?

Nehemiah:
Return and Resurrection

Based on Nehemiah 1-6

It's nice to go home after a long time away. And this is a story about how the people of Israel returned home to the place they loved, Jerusalem, after a long time away.

Years before, the people had been forced out of their houses and taken to foreign lands. But even in those strange places, they still remembered what their homes had been like, and more importantly, they remembered who God was and that they were God's people.

They remembered because God sent special people to look after them and remind them of God's ways. These special people were called prophets. One prophet was named Nehemiah, and he worked in the court of King Artaxerxes (Ahr-tuh-ZURK-seez) of Persia.

Nehemiah had a unique and dangerous job. Because enemies occasionally tried to poison the king, Nehemiah's job was to pour and taste every glass of the king's wine first, making sure it was safe to drink.

Because he risked his life every day to look after the king, the king trusted and liked Nehemiah. One day, when Nehemiah came into the king's dinner chamber looking sad, the king asked him, "Why are you so sad? I know you are not sick, or you wouldn't be here. This can only be sadness of the heart. What is troubling you?"

"I am grieving my beloved Jerusalem," said Nehemiah. "Why should I not be sad when the city—the place of my ancestors' graves—is destroyed, and its gates have been destroyed by fire?"

Like a friend as much as a king, Artaxerxes said, "What do you need?"

"If it pleases you," said Nehemiah, "and if I have served you well, I ask that you send me to Judah, where my people lived and where Solomon built God's temple. I want to rebuild the walls around the city."

Now Artaxerxes of Persia was a good king. Persia had conquered Babylonia—the same empire that had demolished Jerusalem in war. God helped Artaxerxes understand that Nehemiah's desire to restore his homeland was a good thing. And so Artaxerxes said that he would help.

"How long will you be gone?" asked the king. "And what do you need?"

Like a waterfall unfreezing on the first day of spring, Nehemiah's heart rejoiced. "Safe passage, and enough timber to make the walls of Jerusalem strong once more!" replied Nehemiah.

With a promise for as much timber as he needed, Nehemiah rode into Jerusalem on one of the king's majestic horses, surrounded by royal officers, to rebuild his beloved city.

It wasn't always easy. Even though the temple itself, the one that King Solomon had built, was being restored to its former glory after years of warfare, old enemies wanted to block the complete restoration of Jerusalem. An all-powerful God was too much for them. Two men in particular, Sanballat the Horonite and Tobiah the Ammonite, vowed to keep the wall from being rebuilt and spied on Nehemiah from dawn to dusk.

But Nehemiah's years of being the wine taster for the king had made him strong and clever. Knowing he was being followed by spies during the daylight hours, Nehemiah rode out and toured the city and its broken walls by night.

And then he rallied his fellow Israelites to trust in God's word of hope—the promise to rebuild Jerusalem—despite any objections.

"Jerusalem lies in ruins with its gates buried," he told them. "But God is on our side. He has never left us! Come, let us rebuild the walls to our great city!"

The people shouted, "Yes! We have waited for this moment! Let us begin now!"

Directed by Nehemiah, each family took responsibility for rebuilding part of the wall. Pound. Stack. Level. Thump. Hammer. Like an oak sapling growing into a sturdy tree, the wall became healthy and strong once more.

The naysayers, Sanballat and Tobiah, tried to derail the workers by making fun of the project. "Those walls are so puny! Should one little fox run across its top, the whole thing will crumble! It looks like a little squirrel house," taunted Sanballat. "It's a doll house!" shouted Tobiah.

But Nehemiah did not answer. Instead, he prayed and placed guards at the wall day and night to protect the workers. Half of the crew did manual labor while the other half watched over them, holding spears, shields, bows, and armor.

Sanballat and Tobiah continued to make fun of Nehemiah and the workers. They tried to trick Nehemiah to come down to where they could hurt him.

"We just want to talk to you," they said. "Come down to this nice, friendly park, and let's chat." They even threatened to send a false report to the king: "Nehemiah is saying that he's God!"

But Nehemiah wasn't saying he was God; he wasn't fooled or scared. He knew that God wanted him to finish repairing the wall, and he stuck to it. When construction was done, Artaxerxes made Nehemiah the governor of Jerusalem. And "governor" was a good word, for Nehemiah understood that God was the one who was really in charge and that Nehemiah was God's helper in governing the the land.

Nehemiah also knew that walls were not enough to keep a city strong. For that, the Word of God was needed. One day, Nehemiah and all the citizens of Jerusalem gathered for a solemn reading of the law, or as it is better known, the Torah, by a wise man named Ezra. Through this reading of the first five books of the Bible, the people heard both their sacred history and the rules that God had set down for how they should live in the world. So much had been forgotten over the years; so much had been lost.

Nehemiah took care of rebuilding the walls. Ezra reminded people of who they were, and God gave them hope and strength once again.

And thank goodness Nehamiah rebuilt Jerusalem, for it would become a very special place for Jesus. As he grew up, Jesus fell in love with Jerusalem, the city that had meant so much to his ancestors. When he was eight days old, an old woman named Anna and an old man named Simeon recognized him as the Messiah at the temple in Jerusalem. When he was only twelve, Jesus began instructing his elders on everything he knew about God and scripture. As a faithful Jewish man, Jesus returned to Jerusalem each year on Passover to celebrate the night that God had led the people of Israel out of slavery in Egypt. And when Jesus died and came back to life, it happened in his beloved city of Jerusalem.

Reflection Questions

- How do you feel when you come home after a long time away? How do you think the Israelites felt when they came home to Jerusalem?

- Nehemiah used his skills of planning, measuring, and inspiring others to get the wall built. What are the skills that you bring to projects?

- Rebuilding Jerusalem wasn't a one-person job; everyone needed to work together. Describe a time when you had to work together with others to do something you couldn't do alone. What was that experience like?

Jesus, Mary, & Gabriel

Based on Luke 1

Picture yourself in a warm snuggly blanket. But this isn't just any blanket. This special blanket makes you invisible so that you can listen to one of the greatest conversations in history. There you are, tucked into the corner of a small house in Nazareth (NAZ-er-uth) about 2,000 years ago. You are not alone. A girl is there, sweeping the dirt floor in the house. Her long, dark hair swings as she sweeps.

Every so often she twirls around, holding her broom like an imaginary dance partner. You can hear her humming, but as the light grows dim in the room, she stops. She spots the same thing you do: a large figure in the doorway, stooping to get his wings through the door.

Wait a minute. His WINGS? People don't have wings. Only angels have wings. This can only mean one thing. It's an angel!

"Greetings, Mary," says the angel. **"The Lord is with you."**

You can almost see Mary thinking: *What?*

"Do not be afraid, Mary," says the angel.

Yet Mary is afraid. After all, usually people come in the door: mothers and fathers and siblings. But angels?

"You have found favor with God," says the angel. Mary's jaw drops open.

"You will conceive and bear a son, and you will name him Jesus. He will be great, and he will be called the Son of the Most High."

A baby?

"But how can this be?" says Mary. **"I have no husband."**

"The Holy Spirit will come over you," says the angel. **"You will conceive and bear a son and call him Jesus. He will be great and will be called the Son of the Most High. God will give him the throne of his ancestor David, and he will reign over the house of Jacob forever. Of his kingdom there will be no end."**

Now your mind is whirling. This is a lot to take in. There's a choice to be made, and it's up to Mary. The angel waits. You wait. The decision is Mary's. Either way, it will be momentous.

Then, shoulders back, Mary steps forward. Looking the angel in the eyes, she says: **"Here am I, the servant of the Lord. Let it be with me according to your word."**

With a joyful fluttering of wings, the angel turns and leaves—but not before he looks in your direction.

"I'm counting on you, Mary. And I'm also counting on your friend over there to help spread the word about Jesus."

Ah, God's angels can see through special blankets, it appears. When you poke your head out so that Mary can see you, she smiles as well—for she now has a friend.

"Come with me," Mary says.

And so you do. Mary is excited, but she is also scared. In those days, having a baby before marriage often brought terrible punishment. So Mary travels to the hill country outside of Nazareth to stay with her older cousin, Elizabeth, who is also pregnant.

You've heard the word "holy," mostly used in church. But when you see Mary step into Elizabeth's house, you see a wonderful holy moment. A tiny older woman, Elizabeth's face lights up like a firecracker when she sees her young cousin.

The Holy Spirit fills Elizabeth as she shouts, **"You are blessed, special, chosen by God to carry a holy baby in your body! As soon as I saw you, the baby in me leaped for joy. You are incredibly faithful, because you have believed all that God has promised you."**

For days, Mary has been wondering and worrying. Did she really see an angel, or was it all a crazy dream? How would she explain all of this to Joseph? What does it mean that God has chosen her, of all people, to carry God into the world?

When Mary hears Elizabeth speak, she knows that everything will be all right. Elizabeth's words remind her that this is all God's plan, and God is the one in control. Mary's heart fills with joy, and she bursts into song:

"My soul magnifies the Lord,
and my spirit rejoices in God my Savior,
for he has looked with favor on the lowliness of his servant.
Surely, from now on all generations will call me blessed;
for the Mighty One has done great things for me,
and holy is his name.

His mercy is for those who fear him
from generation to generation.
He has shown strength with his arm;
he has scattered the proud in the thoughts of their hearts.

He has brought down the powerful from their thrones,
and lifted up the lowly;
he has filled the hungry with good things,
and sent the rich away empty.

He has helped his servant Israel,
in remembrance of his mercy,
according to the promise he made to our ancestors,
to Abraham and to his descendants forever."

Mary's song of joy is so special that it echoes through the ages. Christians around the world still sing it today, joining our voices to Mary's in her *Magnificat*. As we sing, we are reminded that God calls to us, just as he did to Mary all those years ago. Mary's extraordinary answer of yes to God changed the whole world. And each of us is given the choice to be like Mary, offering a humble and joyful yes whenever God calls us to serve.

When Mary's baby boy, Jesus, is born in Bethlehem nine months later, shepherds gather around the manger, their hearts overflowing with joy. Joseph, Mary's husband, stands by his wife and newborn son, his face beaming with pride and love. Stars blaze in the heavens, brighter than ever before, particularly one special star, sent to light the way. Wise men from far away arrive with gifts. And angels are everywhere, singing praises and thanking God that Jesus has been born. Because this baby, born in a manger, is God made flesh, love in human form.

Reflection Questions

- Imagine being Mary and hearing about God's plan. How do you think she felt? How would you feel?

- Mary had a choice to do what God asked or to say no. Why is it important to know that she had a choice?

- What do you know about angels? What do you imagine angels look like?

- Mary sang a song of joy and praise to God, which is sometimes called the *Magnificat*. What do you notice about her song? What do you say to God when you are happy?

Jesus & His Friends

Based on Matthew 3, 4, 8

That little baby born in a manger grew up. As he grew older, Jesus became wiser and stronger, and the way that he talked and the way that he lived reflected the image and glory of God. When Jesus was about thirty years old, he heard that his cousin John the Baptist was baptizing people in the Jordan River. Crowds of people were coming to confess their sins, receive forgiveness, wash in the water, and make a new start at life.

People wanted to be close to God, close to heaven. And so they came from Jerusalem and all over Judea, from the towns along the Jordan and the countryside.

"Repent, for the kingdom of heaven has come near!" John cried out. "I will baptize you with water, but there is one who is more powerful than me. He will baptize you with the Holy Spirit and with fire."

John did not expect Jesus to show up on the banks of the river, asking to be baptized!

"I am not worthy to carry your sandals," John said to Jesus. "You should be baptizing me!"

But Jesus insisted and was baptized by John. When Jesus came up from the water, a dove flew down and sat on his shoulder. It was the spirit of God, and a voice from heaven said: "This is my beloved Son, with whom I am well pleased!"

You might think that Jesus would have started teaching and preaching and doing miracles right away. But Jesus' first action after his baptism was to go off by himself into the wilderness, for forty days and nights to think about all that had happened to him. There, he was tempted by the devil.

Knowing that Jesus was fasting, which means not eating food, the devil offered him food.

"If you are really the Son of God," Satan said, "command these stones to become loaves of bread."

Jesus was so hungry! He so would have liked nothing more than warm bread and tasty cheese to fill his stomach. But because he was training himself to be strong, Jesus said no.

"One does not live by bread alone," Jesus said to Satan, "but by every word that comes from God's mouth."

Satan tried again to make Jesus sin by flying him up to the highest mountain on earth, where he could see all the kingdoms of the world.

"All this I will give you," said Satan, "if you will only fall down and worship me."

"Away with you, Satan!" said Jesus. "God tells us that we must worship only him."

God sent angels to minister to Jesus, and the devil fled.

After forty days and nights, Jesus returned to Nazareth, his hometown. Like he always did on the Sabbath, Jesus went to the synagogue to worship God. When he stood up to read, he was handed a scroll from the prophet Isaiah. Unrolling it, Jesus found words he knew by heart:

"The Spirit of the Lord is upon me,
because he has anointed me
to bring good news to the poor.

He has sent me to proclaim release to the captives
and recovery of sight to the blind,
to let the oppressed go free,

to proclaim the year of the Lord's favor."

All of the people in synagogue looked at Jesus: Something was different about him, something they could not quite define.

"Today this scripture has been fulfilled in your hearing!" Jesus said, and he sat down.

Some of those gathered marveled at his wisdom. Others asked, "Who does he think he is? Is this not Joseph's son?" Others thought Jesus was claiming to be God, and they chased him out of town.

Jesus could have traveled the countryside by himself, preaching and teaching and healing people. But that would have been a lonely life; everyone needs friends and helpers.

Jesus knew he needed strong people; he would be doing a lot of walking and sleeping under the stars. He also knew he needed to be friends with people who would love God, tell the truth, and who would care for the sick and lonely. Walking by the Sea of Galilee one early morning, Jesus saw two fishermen, Simon and his brother, Andrew, casting a net into the sea.

Jesus said to them, "Follow me, and I will make you fish for people!" Immediately they left their nets and followed him. A little farther down the beach, Jesus saw his cousins: James and John, the sons of Zebedee. As soon as Jesus called to them, they left their boat and followed him.

Soon twelve men had given up their regular jobs to follow and help Jesus: Simon Peter, Andrew, James, John, Philip, Bartholomew, Thomas, Matthew, James, Thaddeus, Simon, and Judas. Jesus was also joined in his work by a number of women, including Mary Magdalene, Susanna, Joanna, and Mary, his mother.

Jesus traveled throughout Galilee, teaching people about God and curing disease and sickness. Blind people were given sight. People who couldn't walk were able to dance with joy. Sad people were given the gift of happiness, and even people who had died were brought back to life.

Doing such work was exhausting, even for Jesus. He did not have a cozy home to return to each evening. Jesus and his friends stayed on the road, looking for people who would listen to the good news about God's love.

One night Jesus and his friends climbed into a boat to cross the Sea of Galilee. Jesus was especially tired, and he fell asleep, curled up on a pillow in the back of the boat. His friends, after all, were experienced fishermen. Surely he should be able to catch a few hours of sleep. But the wind and water had other plans. A storm blew in.

Like a cat with a mouse, wave after wave tossed the little boat up and down, threatening to dump Jesus and the others headfirst into the cold water. With water crashing in from all sides, the disciples feared they would drown.

"Lord, wake up!" they cried. **"We are perishing! Save us!"**

Roused from his deep sleep, Jesus said, **"What are you afraid of, you of little faith?"**

Then Jesus got up and told the winds and the sea to calm down—and they did!

The disciples were amazed, saying, **"What sort of man is this, that even the winds and the sea obey him?"**

Reflection Questions

- Baptism means that we are marked as God's own children forever through water and the Holy Spirit. What do you know about the day of your baptism? Ask your parents and godparents about the day that you were baptized. Or, if you haven't been baptized, talk to your parents or priest to learn more about baptism.

- Satan tempts Jesus to do things that he knows are wrong. When have you stood up for what you knew was right? What was that like?

- Jesus has friends and followers who pray with him, eat with him, and work with him. Who are some of the people who help you love and serve God?

Miracles and More

Picture yourself by the Sea of Galilee, in the ancient town of Capernaum [Kuh-PUR-ney-uhm], early one summer morning. You're there with a growing crowd of people, as Jesus' boat is coming into sight. You can't wait to see Jesus in person—and neither can the hundreds of people lining up with you on the shore.

An old woman, crippled and hunched over, hopes Jesus will help her stand tall. A young father, blind since birth, wants his sight restored. A group of four people carry in their friend, wrapped in blankets and too sick to walk, suffering from a dangerously high fever.

All long for the healing touch of Jesus. All want to be whole. And from what you've heard, that's what Jesus wants for everyone as well.

The boat pulls up. The crowd presses in, pushing you forward, so much so that you are standing right next to the boat, with water up to your knees. Four strong, suntanned men jump off to tie down the small craft. And then a man in the boat stands up, a man who has the kindest face you have ever seen. Casting his eyes over the crowd, he sees you—and an unimaginably deep sense of warmth flows through you.

"Jesus, let me give you a hand," says one of the men on the boat, stretching out his hand to help Mister Kind Eyes jump to the shore.

It's Jesus! The one everyone is talking about!

Jesus sees the old crippled woman and puts a hand under her chin. Her back straightens until she is tall and sound—and you swear she skips home to surprise her family. Jesus spots the blind father and reaches out to touch his eyes; they fill with tears when he sees his wife and children for the first time. Kneeling beside the man who has been carried by his friends, Jesus brushes his forehead with the lightest touch, and the sick man stands tall, folds the blanket, and throws his arms around his friends.

Hour after hour, Jesus listens to people tell him their stories, and he reaches out: blessing, praying, counseling. Sometimes just a word is needed. Other times a slight touch will do.

Over the next few months, Jesus comes and goes from town to town, most often without telling people where he is going next. One day he walks through town, then heads to a favorite place of his:

the hills outside Capernaum. You ask your mother if you can follow Jesus, for it seems as if the whole town is starting the trek up the valley. She throws some food in a basket and joins you.

It's a day of healing and of listening. You feel as if you could stay here forever, listening to Jesus teach about God's kingdom. His words nestle deep in your heart.

Jesus says,

"Blessed are those who depend completely on God;
They live, even now, in the kingdom of heaven.

Blessed are those who are sad;
God will tend and comfort them.

Blessed are those who give, instead of take;
God will give them all that they need.

Blessed are those who are hungry and thirsty for what is right;
Their lives and hearts will be full.

Blessed are those who work to forgive, instead of punishing;
God will be gentle and forgiving to them.

Blessed are those with pure hearts;
They will see God always.

Blessed are the peacemakers;
They are true children of God."

Next, Jesus tells some of his parables—little stories with big points.

Jesus tells a story about a tiny mustard seed that grows to be a strong tree with many branches, giving protection and food to many creatures. You listen and wonder whether God's kingdom could be planted and grow in someone small, like you.

Jesus tells a story about a man who loses a sheep and goes to search for it and a story about a woman who loses a coin and tries desperately to find it. And you realize that Jesus never wants anyone to be lost, and God searches desperately for everyone who wanders away.

And then Jesus tells a story about a farmer who throws seed on both rocky soil and good soil, but the seeds only grow in the soil that is rich and ready. You realize that Jesus wants you to be like healthy soil—ready to receive and fully share God's love.

Jesus is not like anyone you've ever heard talk before—and you, like everyone else, feel as if you could spend days, even weeks listening to him.

As the sun begins to cast long shadows, you can see that Jesus is tired—and so are the thousands of people who have filled the hillsides. Jesus' friends glance around, realizing that everyone is getting hungry and tired.

"Time to send everyone home," the disciples say. "It's getting late, and they have no food."

"They do not have to go away," says Jesus. "Give them something to eat."

You can almost see what Jesus' friends are thinking. *Are you crazy? We have no ovens, no stores, no money, no gardens. How are we to produce food for over 5,000 people?*

"Go," says Jesus. "Find food. Now."

One of the disciples, Andrew, notices your basket. "How much food do you have there?" he asks.

"Five barley loaves and two fish," answers your mother.

Andrew goes back to Jesus, pointing at you. And Jesus looks at you and motions, asking without words if you will share your dinner from the basket. You nod, "Yes."

Jesus takes the bread and fish that you have brought and holds them high, asking God's blessing. The loaves and fish are passed around…and there is more than enough for everybody! Everyone eats their fill. And when Jesus asks the disciples to pick up all the crumbs of bread and broken pieces of fish, there are twelve baskets of leftovers.

What a day! You have just witnessed the miracle that Christians everywhere will talk about and marvel over for years and years. They'll call it "The Feeding of the Five Thousand." And you were part of it.

There is so much to think and talk about with your mother as you walk home. Your heart and your stomach both feel very, very full. You have learned that Jesus can do anything and that he cares about —and takes care of—people who come to him for healing. And you understand that Jesus wants to feed everyone, not just with bread and fishes for their stomachs but with love to fill their hearts.

Reflection Questions

- Jesus loves to tell stories. What are some of your favorite stories to hear and to tell? Which of Jesus' stories do you like best, and why?

- The child in the story shared food so that everyone could eat. How does God ask you to share what you have with others?

- Some people call this story the miracle of the loaves and fishes. Which parts of the story do you think are miracles?

- Describe any miracles that you might have seen or heard about. Have you ever experienced a miracle in your own life?

Sometimes the only way to understand a sad event is to walk right up to it, look at it, and talk about it with people we love. And that's the way it is with the end of Jesus' earthly life. Jesus died a tragic death, and while it is sad to think about, Christians tell the story because it is also the story of how much God loves us.

What's important is that the story doesn't stay sad forever. God helped Jesus do something that no one had ever done before—or since: to rise from the dead, fully alive, so that he could always be with us.

But first, the sad part.

Every year, Jesus went to Jerusalem with thousands of other Jews to celebrate Passover, the night that God, with Moses' assistance, helped the Jewish people escape from slavery in Egypt. Like other Jews, Jesus said special prayers and ate a special meal, thanking God for freedom and a new land of their own.

While Jesus was eating the Passover meal with his twelve disciples, his face grew surprisingly serious. **"One of you will betray me,"** Jesus said. His friends were stunned. Voices from around the room clamored to be heard.

"Is it me?" said one.

"Surely not I, Lord!" cried another.

"The one who has dipped his hand into the bowl with me will betray me," Jesus said. **"And it would be better for that man if he had not been born."**

Like an Arctic blast, a cold silence filled the room. And then a voice from Judas, the man seated next to him. **"Surely not I, Teacher?"**

"You have said so," said Jesus.

Jesus' circle of trust had been broken. Things would never be the same again.

Jesus reached for the bread on the table. "Take this and eat it," he said. "This is my body." And then Jesus held up a glass of wine. After thanking God, Jesus blessed it and said, "Drink from it, all of you, for this is my blood which is poured out for the forgiveness of sins."

The disciples did not always understand what Jesus was trying to tell them, but they knew how much he loved them. So they did what he said: They ate the bread and drank the wine that he gave them. Later Jesus went out to pray at the Mount of Olives, and they followed him. Judas had fled, and he was not with the group.

Oh, it was hard for the disciples to stay awake! Sometimes grief causes people to fall asleep, and that was what happened with the disciples. Jesus finished his prayers and went to wake his friends.

"Come, it is time to be going," Jesus said, "for the hour is at hand."

But Jesus' safe departure was not to happen. Blocking the exit from the garden was Judas, the one who would betray Jesus. And standing with Judas was a large group of Roman soldiers. Whispering to the soldiers, Judas said, "The one whom I will kiss is the man; arrest him."

Then Judas came to Jesus and said, "Greetings, Teacher," and kissed him.

"Do what you are here to do," Jesus said.

Jesus was arrested and carried off to face the Roman authorities, including Pontius Pilate, the governor. Miracles and special teachings and stories were not something Pilate understood. When Pilate asked Jesus to explain himself, Jesus said nothing. Pilate did not know God, and because he thought of Jesus as a dangerous troublemaker, he sentenced Jesus to die.

In those days, criminals were nailed to crosses, so that's what Pilate's soldiers did to Jesus. There weren't many people at the cross. Most of the twelve disciples, except John, were hiding because they were scared. Jesus' mother and some of his women friends, including Mary Magdalene and Salome (Suh-LOH-mee) stood where Jesus could see them. As hard as it was to watch someone they loved die, this small group of women helped Jesus know that he wasn't alone in his last moments.

For three hours Jesus hung on the cross. People have always wondered why Jesus didn't summon an army of angels to come and rescue him. Certainly all of heaven's citizens were waiting, just out of sight, and would have come in a minute if called. But Jesus knew that if were he to walk away, his work of love would be unfinished. It would be like a shepherd leaving his sheep to freeze in the middle of a blinding snowstorm rather than going out, finding them, and bringing them safely home.

Jesus held us close to him as he hung on the cross. After three hours, he died. When he took his last breath, the heavens opened up, and the earth shook.

As you will see in the next chapter, Jesus' death was not the end of the story. In many ways, it was only the beginning. Healing people was what Jesus liked to do the most—and a healing so amazing that it was almost unimaginable was about to begin.

Reflection Questions

- On his last night on earth, Jesus shared a special meal with his friends and spent time in prayer with God. What would you do with your last night?

- At dinner with his friends, Jesus asked them to eat bread and drink wine to remember him. What are some things that you do to remember Jesus?

- Jesus could have come down from the cross, but he didn't. Why do you think he chooses to stay there?

- Some of Jesus' friends were too scared to watch him die. Have you ever been too scared to do something hard? What was that like?

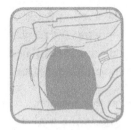

Jesus died and was buried, his body laid in a tomb with a stone rolled in front of the opening. The cross stood empty. The disciples had scattered, full of sadness and fear. It seemed like the end.

And then Sunday morning arrived. Mary Magdalene and her friends moved through the empty streets of Jerusalem with their heads down, clutching spices and special ointments under their warm cloaks. Ready to wrap and prepare Jesus' body for its final return to earth, Mary Magdalene expected death where there had been life, despair where there had been joy.

Today, she would do one of the hardest things in her life: say goodbye to her beloved friend, teacher, and Lord. Jesus had awakened her to a world she thought only belonged to others—a world of love. Mary Magdalene had seen Jesus heal hundreds of people and had been on the road as one of his disciples. Jesus had healed her of seven demons. No longer was she afraid or lonely.

But Mary Magdalene was also a practical woman. On this morning, she and her friends faced what seemed like an insurmountable problem: They needed to move the huge stone blocking the entrance to Jesus' tomb.

How will we manage it? It must weigh a thousand pounds. How can four women move it away when it took a group of muscle-bound soldiers to put it there in the first place?

Rounding the corner, Mary stopped dead in her tracks. The stone had been rolled away.

No! This, on top of everything else? They killed Jesus and now someone has stolen his body? Can't they even let his body rest in peace?

Whirling around, Mary ran back to the house in Jerusalem where Peter and John were staying, grieving Jesus' death.

"They have stolen Jesus out of the tomb, and I don't know where he is!" Mary cried.

Peter and John raced to the tomb. Entering first was Peter, one of Jesus' closest friends, followed by young John. Just as Mary Magdalene had reported, the tomb was empty. No body. No light. Nothing. Only strips of linen that had been wrapped around Jesus' body remained, tossed on the floor like trash. Heads down and hearts broken, the men headed back to town.

Mary Magdalene could have walked away at that moment and followed the men back to Jerusalem. But she didn't. Setting foot in the tomb—where she expected darkness—two angels greeted her. **"Why are you crying?"** they asked.

"Because they have taken away my Lord, and I don't know where he is!"

When Mary said this, she turned around to see a man standing near her. Guessing he was the gardener, she said: **"Sir, if you have carried Jesus away, tell me where you have laid him, so that I might bring him back."**

"Mary!" said the man.

With that one word, everything became clear—amazingly, beautifully, breathtakingly clear.

"Teacher!" cried Mary. It was Jesus talking to her—fully alive.

The power of darkness was broken forever. Evil powers had done their best to try to destroy Jesus, but they had been pushed back. God's love had triumphed. Jesus had overcome death and the grave.

When Mary Magdalene rushed to embrace Jesus, he stepped back.

"Don't cling to me now, Mary. Go and tell my brothers that I am ascending to my Father and your Father, to my God and your God."

So Mary went and announced to the disciples, **"I have seen the Lord!"** And Mary Magdalene —the woman who had been tormented by seven demons—became the apostle to the apostles: the first person to share and proclaim the good news of Jesus' resurrection.

Mary Magdalene was not the only person Jesus would surprise. When it was evening on the first day of the week, ten of the disciples were behind locked doors. Scared because Jesus had been killed—and thinking they might be persecuted themselves—they sat together, not sure of their next move.

Would they disband? Would they slink away, back to their own homes and families? Would they be the butt of jokes or worse, subject to punishment? They had heard reports from Mary Magdalene and others that Jesus had been spotted, but it seemed too good to be true. Risen from the dead? How could that even be possible? Once people died, they stayed dead!

Suddenly, without opening a single door or window, a familiar figure joined them: Jesus!

"Peace be with you," Jesus said. Stunned—and overjoyed—the disciples could barely talk.

"Peace be with you. As the Father has sent me, so I send you." And then Jesus breathed on them, saying, "Receive the Holy Spirit."

But Thomas, one of the twelve, was not with them that day. When the other disciples told him that they had seen Jesus, Thomas was not convinced. "Unless I can see the holes in his hands and put my hand in the hole in his side, I will not believe."

A week later, the disciples were together again; this time Thomas was with them. They were eating and trying to make sense of recent events. Although the doors were shut, Jesus came and stood among them again.

"Peace be with you," Jesus said. And then, stretching out his hands, Jesus looked at Thomas. "Put your fingers here and see my hands. Reach your hand out and touch my side. Do not doubt, but believe."

Thomas was overjoyed. "My Lord and my God!"

"Have you believed because you have seen me?" asked Jesus. "Blessed are those who have not seen and who have come to believe."

For the next forty days, Jesus traveled with his disciples, eating and performing miracles and telling them more about God. And then he rose into heaven. The disciples began the amazing and holy work of telling the whole world about the love of God in the life of Jesus.

Reflection Questions

- How did you feel when you read this story?

- Jesus looks different when he appears to different people. Close your eyes. What does Jesus look like to you?

- Mary Magdalene meets the risen Jesus and immediately runs to tell all her friends about it. How can you share the good news of Jesus with others?

- Thomas has a hard time believing in Jesus' resurrection. Have you ever had a hard time believing? What has helped you believe when you were struggling?

Chapter 21: Filled with the Holy Spirit
The Church is Born
Based on Acts 1, 2, and 9

Have you ever felt something so special that you could almost feel it in your toes? That everything was good and right and that everyone around you was feeling the same way?

The Holy Spirit is like that, and God's gift of the Spirit is what made some of Jesus' friends strong and helped them build the Church. And the Holy Spirit is what keeps the Church going, even today.

Joy filled Peter's heart as he watched Jesus rise into heaven. Since his resurrection from the dead, Jesus had been with Peter and the other disciples for forty days. Now, Jesus was ascending into heaven. Peter knew that Jesus was God's son, but seeing the heavens open up and receive him was a sight unlike any other. Was that God's hand reaching out for Jesus? Were those choirs of angels singing, welcoming him back?

Peter still couldn't believe his good fortune—that he had been one of those in Jesus' inner circle. And as the sky closed, Peter thought of that day when Jesus had singled him out.

"I tell you, you are Peter—Petra—rock!" Jesus had said. **"And on this rock I will build my church, and the gates of Hades will not prevail against it. I will give you the keys of the kingdom of heaven, and whatever you bind on earth will be bound in heaven, and whatever you loose on earth will be loosed in heaven."**

I'll never know what Jesus saw in me, but I won't let him down, thought Peter. *I remember walking on water trying to reach him and almost drowning—but Jesus saved me. All I have to do is reach out when things get tough, and Jesus will be right there, even if I can't see him.*

Days passed. A new disciple, Matthias, was chosen to replace Judas, the one who had betrayed Jesus. And when a special day called Pentecost came—a time when Jews celebrated receiving God's law—the disciples gathered together in one room.

Suddenly, a sound like the rush of a violent wind filled the entire house—and changed everything. It was the Holy Spirit. Sometimes, the Holy Spirit creeps in like fog on little cat feet. Other times, the Holy Spirit moves entire nations. But the day the Holy Spirit first came among the disciples will always be special and set apart, for nothing like it had happened before and nothing like it has happened since.

Without even trying, the disciples started talking in other languages—languages that were brand new to them and to each other—yet they could understand one another! And when they looked around at each other, it looked like they had flames—tongues of fire—coming out of their heads. It was amazing! And later, when people called what they were doing "speaking in tongues," they knew the Holy Spirit was very close to them.

People outside the house where Peter and his friends were staying, devout Jewish men and women who had come to Jerusalem from other countries to celebrate Pentecost, heard the commotion. And when they came inside to see what was going on, they were surprised to find that the disciples were talking about God in all of their languages!

Imagine you are in church on Sunday morning, and the girl on your right suddenly turns and talks to you in German, the boy on your left talks to you in French, and the man ahead speaks in Arabic? And even though you have never studied those languages, you can suddenly understand them all! That's what the day of Pentecost was like.

Peter and the other disciples were filled with the Holy Spirit. The presence of God was with them as they went out into the world, preaching and teaching and helping people in need. They spread the good news about Jesus in words and deeds and taught people how to live together faithfully and worship God fully.

But they were not the only ones who felt God's presence. The Holy Spirit is amazing and powerful. And sometimes it stirs people's hearts so much that they become new people from the inside out.

That's the way the Holy Spirit worked with a man named Saul. He was a smart and educated Jewish man, but he was also a very angry man. Saul hated Christians and hunted down Jesus' followers to put them in jail because he thought they were wrong about Jesus.

But one night, as Saul was traveling to Damascus, a light from heaven flashed around him. As he fell to the ground, he heard a voice say, "Saul, Saul, why do you persecute me?"

And then Saul asked the voice a strange question: "Who are you, Lord?"

"I am Jesus, whom you are persecuting," came the reply. "Get up and enter the city, and you will be told what to do." Saul got up, and although his eyes were open, he could not see. For three days, Saul was without sight, and he neither ate nor drank.

In Damascus, one of Jesus' followers called Ananias also received a message from God. "Ananias, go find a man named Saul on a street called Straight. Lay your hands on him, and bring him back into the fold."

"Are you kidding?" asked Ananias. "Me? That man hates Christians. Why would I want to get near him?"

"Go," said the Lord. "Saul is an instrument whom I have chosen to bring my name before the world. I myself will show him how much he must suffer for the sake of my name."

So Ananias went out into the city, found Saul, and laid his hands on him.

"Brother Saul," he said, "The Lord Jesus, who appeared to you on your way here, has sent me so that you will regain your sight and be filled with the Holy Spirit." And the scales that were covering Saul's eyes fell away, and he could see. Then Saul got up and was baptized.

After eating some food, Saul regained his strength to go on with his journey—but now as a passionate pilgrim for God. As a sign of the change in his life, Saul (which means something like "pushy or boastful") changed his name to Paul (which means "small'). Paul understood that God was doing something very big, and he was now a small but important part of God's work. Paul was ready to travel all over the world, telling people the good news of Jesus that changed his whole life.

Reflection Questions

- Have you ever felt the Holy Spirit working in your life? If so, how? If not, what do you think it would feel like?

- What do you think the Holy Spirit looks like? How would you draw the Holy Spirit?

- God never gives up on us. What does it mean to never give up on someone?

- Saul changed his mind about God, and that changed his life. When have you changed your mind or your life? What was it like?

Building the Body of Christ

Based on Acts 2 and 16

After the scales fell from Paul's eyes, he was a new man. And that's what God has in mind for all of us, not just Paul. Knowing God *should* change us and make us want to go out and share this extraordinary story of God's love for us.

Paul traveled some 10,000 miles telling people the story of Jesus, starting and supporting congregations. He used his energy and passion as Jesus' hands and feet to build the church.

Paul was working in very challenging circumstances. There were no phones or video chats, so Paul talked to people in face to face. There were no airplanes or buses or cars, so he walked on foot or sailed on boats thousands of miles to see and encourage other believers. And since he couldn't call them on the phone or send emails, Paul wrote many letters. Some of the letters—called Epistles—are still read in our churches today.

Paul's life was often in danger—but he kept on preaching God's word, and nothing could stop him. From shipwrecks to jail to beatings and starvation, Paul kept the faith, no matter what hardships came his way.

Paul loved baptizing people—bringing them into God's family. One day, in a little town called Philippi, Paul baptized a woman named Lydia. When Paul told Lydia about Jesus, she was so happy that right away she said, **"Baptize me!"** Then Lydia invited Paul and his friends to use her home as a missionary center.

The very next day though, Paul ran into trouble at the town square. A girl—and we don't know her name—started yelling at Paul. The girl was a slave, and her owners forced her to tell fortunes. Sometimes she could see things that other people couldn't.

One look at Paul told her that he was God's person. Day after day, when she was supposed to be telling fortunes, she would yell: **"He works for the Lord Jesus Christ! He works for the Lord Jesus Christ!"** Paul grew irritated. After all, he had work to do! Little did Paul know that the slave girl was part of that important work. Finally, Paul realized that she was being tormented by demons.

"Demons, in the name of Jesus Christ, come out of that girl!" Paul shouted. The demons obeyed right away, because they were scared of Jesus. Free of demons, the girl sat down, calm and well-mannered.

You would think that freeing someone from demons would be the best gift of all. And it was for the girl. But the slave owners were angry, because the girl had made lots of money for them by telling fortunes. Now they weren't getting any of that extra money. So they had Paul thrown in prison.

Late that night, as Paul and his friends were sitting in their jail cell, a violent earthquake tore through the countryside, springing open the heavy prison gates. The men could have simply walked away. But not Paul. He and his companions chose to stay in their jail cells. They spent the night singing hymns and praying to God. In the morning, Paul and his friends were released and walked out of jail as free men. The jailor was so impressed with their trust in God that he asked Paul to baptize his entire family. Of course, Paul did.

Paul had to leave town quickly because some people still were angry with him. But Paul didn't forget the people he had met in Philippi, the people he had baptized, the people who came to believe in Jesus while he was there, and the slave girl and others he had healed. To encourage and comfort them, Paul wrote them letters, which they would read aloud when they gathered to pray and worship. One of the letters that Paul wrote to the Philippians said this:

"I love you and want to see you. You bring me joy and make me proud of you. Continue following the Lord as I have told you. Be full of joy in the Lord always. I will say again, be full of joy. Let all men see that you are gentle and kind. The Lord is coming soon. Do not worry about anything. But pray and ask God for everything you need. And when you pray, always give thanks. And God's peace will keep your hearts and minds in Christ Jesus. The peace that God gives is so great that we cannot understand it" (Philippians 4:1b, 4-7).

After Paul left Philippi, he continued to travel, preaching and teaching about Jesus. After he left, Paul sent letters back to each church, letters of teaching and encouragement, letters of concern and care.

When the people of Corinth wondered how to show Jesus to the world, Paul wrote them a letter, telling them that the best way to teach people about God is to love them fully and completely, the way that God loves. **"Love is patient and kind. Love is not jealous, it does not brag, and it is not proud. Love is not rude, is not selfish, and does not become angry easily. Love does not remember wrongs done against it. Love takes no pleasure in evil, but rejoices over the truth. Love patiently accepts all things. It always trusts, always hopes, and always continues strong"** (1 Corinthians 13:4-7).

When the people in the church in Galatia were arguing about who belonged to God and who didn't, Paul wrote to remind them that we are all brothers and sisters, children of God, saying, **"Now, in Christ, there is no difference between Jew and Greek. There is no difference between slaves and free men. There is no difference between male and female. You are all the same in Christ Jesus"** (Galatians 3:28).

And when the people in Rome were worried about whether they would always be close to God, Paul wrote a letter to comfort them, saying, **"Yes, I am sure that nothing can separate us from the love God has for us. Not death, not life, not angels, not ruling spirits, nothing now, nothing in the future, no powers, nothing above us, nothing below us, or anything else in the whole world will ever be able to separate us from the love of God that is in Christ Jesus our Lord"** (Romans 8:38-39).

Paul's letters to his friends and fellow Christians were so important that people kept them, saving them like precious treasures. They passed them down from mother to daughter, from grandfather to grandson. We have copies of Paul's letters, and we read them aloud in our churches today, just as they were read aloud in some of the very first churches.

Listen for Paul's words this week in your church. If you try hard, you just might be able to see Paul in your mind's eye, pointing the way to the one he loved more than anything else—Jesus.

Reflection Questions

- What do you imagine happened to the fortune-telling slave girl? What might she have done with her life?

- Paul wrote letters encouraging people in their faith. Have you ever written or received a letter of encouragement? How did it help you?

- Paul stayed in jail even after he had been set free so that he could tell people about Jesus. How might we follow his example?

- Paul teaches us about how to live a life of faith. Which of his teachings is your favorite? Which one do you think is the hardest?

Teaching and Preaching

Based on James 1-3; 1 Timothy 4:6-21;
2 Timothy 1:5; and Philippians 2:19-23

Paul was an important leader of the early Christians, traveling far and wide and starting churches in many different places. But Paul wasn't the only leader in the early church. In fact, as the good news about Jesus spread, more and more people wanted to follow Jesus, and Christians began to gather all over the world.

In each community, leaders rose up—people with special gifts for preaching and teaching, people who made the stories of the Bible come alive. One of those teachers was a man named James.

James sat with his pen (quill) in his hand, staring at the sky. Even though he knew he was doing the right thing by traveling far from home to preach and teach about Jesus, James missed his friends and his fellow followers of Jesus. James had just received a letter, full of news from his friends and full of questions about Jesus. People wanted to know how they could live out their faith in their daily lives—what it looked like to follow Jesus at home and school and work, while eating and sleeping and playing. James asked God to give him wisdom and strength, and then he started writing:

"Dear friends,

"I don't have all the answers, but I do know this. We can't just talk about our faith; we have to live it out loud. Listen to the words of Jesus. Listen to the stories of the Bible. It's important to learn about your faith. But don't stop there. Don't just be hearers of God's word, be people who do God's work in the world.

"Be a good listener. Be slow to anger and quick to forgive—just like God is.

"Be careful about what you say. Words can be dangerous. Unkind words can burn people, like a fire. The way we speak to other people should be like the way that we speak to God: using words of blessing and praise and love, not words that are ugly and hurtful. Everyone makes mistakes sometimes. But we should practice speaking kindly, saying things that build people up instead of tearing them down.

"Treat everyone equally. Don't judge people by what they look like or what they are wearing. Don't treat rich people better than poor people. God loves everyone

equally, and you should too. Jesus said to 'love your neighbor as yourself.' God reminds us that we are all neighbors, all children of God. So love everyone.

"And don't just say that you love someone. Show it. Live lives of love.

"When you see someone without clothes who is cold, or someone without food who is hungry, it's not enough to say, 'I'll pray for you, God's peace be with you.' Real faith is about action. Give clothes to the cold and food to the hungry. You have more than enough; share what you have. True faith looks like this: feeding the hungry, clothing the naked, caring for orphans and widows, protecting the vulnerable, and giving companionship to the lonely.

"Show with your lives what you proclaim with your lips. Show people the heart of God, which is pure, peaceful, gentle, forgiving, patient, and accepting.

"Friends, I know that this is hard. It is hard to put our faith into action. It is easier to sit back and do nothing. It is hard to speak kindly when you are angry. It is easier to just say what you are thinking. It is hard to love everyone. It is easier to just love the people that we like, the people who seem like us. But we can do hard things. God promises to be with us, to hear us when we pray, and to love us no matter what. And God gives us one another, brothers and sisters in God's family, to encourage each other, teach each other, and support each other."

As soon as he finished his letter, James rolled up the scroll and sent it off to his friends. James prayed that his words might encourage the people who read it. He also said a quick prayer that he would have the strength and courage to be someone who lived his faith in Jesus—not someone who just talked about it.

James was one of many preachers and teachers traveling around and spreading the message of Jesus to the ends of the earth. Others—men and women, old and young, from all different backgrounds and places—were excited about Jesus and wanted to tell the world about him. One of those teachers was a young man named Timothy, a student of Paul.

Timothy was thinking about his Grandma Lois as he walked through the streets on his way to the church gathering. Grandma Lois and Timothy's mom, Eunice, had taught him about Jesus since he was a small boy. They had heard Paul and his friend Silas preach in Lystra where they lived, and they immediately asked to be baptized and join the followers of Jesus.

Timothy remembered his grandmother's huge smile as she talked about the love of Jesus. He remembered how she would recite the words of the scriptures again and again, until everyone in his house knew the holy words by heart. And he remembered the tender way that Lois would prepare extra bread for those in the church who were hungry, sharing what she had, even when she had very little. Yes, Grandma Lois taught Timothy much about the love of Jesus.

And Timothy knew, even when he was little, that he was called to follow Jesus too. So he did—studying the scriptures carefully, serving the poor lovingly, preaching the gospel passionately. Timothy became a leader in his church as a teenager. And when Paul came back to town, he asked Timothy to come with him, traveling all around the world to tell people about the love of Jesus.

Timothy was nervous. He was scared to leave home, and he didn't really like to talk in front of big crowds. But he loved Jesus with all his heart, and Timothy wanted other people to know about all that Jesus had said and done. So off he went.

Timothy could remember that first long journey to Macedonia—the way the ship rocked on the waves, the taste of the salt spray of the water on his lips. From there, Timothy went with Paul to Ephesus and Corinth. In each place, Timothy taught and preached about Jesus. And he helped Paul write many letters—letters of encouragement and instruction to the people of Corinth and Philippi and Colossia.

And now, here Timothy was, walking to the house where the followers of Jesus gathered to eat and pray and sing. Paul was off elsewhere, but he had entrusted Timothy with these people, with this church. They wanted to hear the scriptures explained. They wanted to share in the breaking of bread, remembering Jesus' last meal with his disciples. They wanted to hear the good news of God in Christ, and it was Timothy's turn to tell them. Timothy was nervous, as he always was. He was so young; would people respect him? He wasn't always the best speaker; would people listen to him?

But as Timothy walked, he remembered what Paul had written to him, **"Do not let anyone look down on you because you are young. Even a young person can set an example for other believers: by loving fully, living compassionately, speaking kindly, and following Jesus faithfully, no matter what."** With God's help, Timothy thought, *I can do that.* So he squared his shoulders and stepped inside.

Reflection Questions

- James told people that it was important not only to talk about Jesus but also to show people the love of Jesus with the way they lived their lives. What are some ways that you can show people Jesus at school or at home?

- James was an encourager; he wrote letters to help encourage people in their faith. How can you encourage your friends and family to follow Jesus more fully?

- Timothy's grandmother taught him to love and serve Jesus. Who are some people who have taught you about Jesus? What have you learned from them?

- Some people didn't think Timothy should be a teacher in the church because he was very young. Has anyone ever told you that you were too young to do something? How did that make you feel?

A New Heaven and A New Earth

Based on Revelation 1, 4-5, 7, and 21-22

Have you ever seen something that no one else could see? A long time ago, on the island of Patmos, a man named John saw something that no one else could see. It was a vision—a revelation—that John believed came straight from God. And even though no one else could see what John saw, he didn't want to keep this vision to himself. As soon as he could, John wrote down everything that he had seen and heard, using words to paint wonderful pictures so that others could imagine what John had seen with his eyes.

John's visions were especially important to the early Church, because those first years after Jesus ascended into heaven were scary times to be a Christian. The Roman Empire persecuted people for following Jesus. Some Christians were jailed for just talking about Jesus. Some were even killed for their faith. John himself had been sent to prison on the faraway island of Patmos as punishment for being a Christian.

Living in such stressful days made people ask big questions: *Was God still in charge? Would good really overcome evil? Would Jesus come back as he promised?*

John was wondering about just these kinds of questions, when Jesus appeared to him in a vision, shining in glory. This is what John saw and heard:

I looked, and I saw the door of heaven standing open.

And there, in heaven, there was a throne, the most beautiful throne you could ever imagine. It looked like it was covered in jewels and wrapped in a rainbow. In front of the throne was a sea of glass, like crystal. And on the throne was Jesus—beautiful, beloved Jesus.

Around the throne were four amazing animals, unlike anything I'd ever seen. They looked like animals in storybooks, covered in wings and with many eyes. These creatures were beautiful and also a bit scary. The animals around the throne were singing, day and night, without ever stopping. They sang, "Holy, holy, holy Lord, God of power and might!"

Around the throne were other rulers, sitting on smaller thrones with crowns on their heads. But those rulers took off their crowns and laid them down before God's throne; they fell on their faces and joined in the singing, praising God with their songs.

I could hear the voices of angels, as they joined the animals and the rulers in song. They sang with their full voices and with all their hearts, "Jesus is the one who is worthy to receive power and glory and honor and blessing."

And in that moment, just when I thought the singing couldn't be any louder or more beautiful, it was. Because every creature in heaven and on the earth and under the earth and in the sea—every creature that God had ever made—joined in the singing too. The walls shook, the whole earth shook, and heaven shook. My ears were filled with songs too beautiful to hear, and my heart was filled to bursting with joy and praise.

And even that was not the end. Because suddenly there were people everywhere. More people than any person could ever count. People of every country and color and language and age and size and shape. Every person was different, and yet every person was wearing the same robe, a white robe, and each of them joined in the song, saying, "God is the one who saves us, and Jesus is the Lamb of God!"

John had never been more joyful than he was at that moment. Everything was right in heaven and on earth because everything was focused on praising and loving God.

But that was only one part of John's vision. He saw other things too. John saw some things that were sad and scary—visions of people turning away from God, images of what happens when people let violence and hatred rule in their hearts instead of love.

But even in the midst of the darkest and scariest things he saw, John heard the voice of Jesus and saw the presence of God. And on the other side of sadness, God gave John a vision of great joy. God showed John his vision of the earth, of all creation, made new.

I looked, and I saw a new heaven and a new earth. Coming down from heaven, I saw a new city, the new Jerusalem. The city was full of light, shining brightly with the glory of God. The walls of the city looked like they were made with jewels: emeralds and sapphires and rubies and turquoise and every kind of precious stone, colorful and precious. The city had twelve gates that were like giant pearls. But the gates were never closed; they always stood open.

The city was full of light, even though there was no sun or moon or any lamps. Instead, God was the light of the city—God's love and glory filled the city so much that it shone more brightly than you could ever imagine. God's presence filled the city; it was everywhere.

I saw a river flowing through the city. It was the river of life, with water as clear as crystal, sparkling like a diamond.

And I heard the voice of Jesus, loud and gentle, coming from the throne. He said, "This water is a gift, my gift, to anyone who is thirsty."

And in that moment of glorious vision I knew: God's home is with all of us. He will wipe every tear from our eyes. Someday there will be no more death, no more grief or crying or pain. All things will be made new, through the power and glory of God.

"I am coming very soon!" Jesus said. And I answered him, with a strong and true voice: "Yes Lord Jesus—please come!"

Before John's vision ended, an angel told him to write down everything he had seen and heard so that others might catch a small glimpse of God's promise and power.

John did his best. He tried to write down what he had seen, even though he didn't understand most of it. He searched for the right words to describe the colors and the sounds and the smells, even though they were unlike anything in this world. Like a poet trying to capture the smell of the forest at night or a composer crafting music to express joy and excitement, John did his best to describe the indescribable, to explain the unexplainable.

John's words brought comfort and strength to all those who were suffering, waiting for Jesus to come, waiting…waiting. And those same words bring comfort and strength to us, while we, like John, wait for Jesus to return.

Reflection Questions

- Have you ever seen something no one else could see or had a dream that seemed very real? What was it?

- What is your favorite thing about John's vision? Why is it your favorite?

- In Revelation, John describes his vision of heaven. Close your eyes and imagine heaven. What does it look like? What does it sound like?

- In John's vision, everyone in heaven is singing songs, praising God. What is your favorite song to sing to praise God?

Going into the World

Congratulations for reading through this whole book of Bible stories! Which stories were your favorites? Were there any you didn't like? Who were your favorite Bible people? What did you learn about God?

Do you remember reading about being with God during the first days of creation and snuggling under his arm as he created the world? Here's the thing: God has always snuggled you in his heart, long before you were born. Even though there are billions of people in this world, God knows you better than anyone else and loves you more than you can imagine.

One of the reasons that Jesus liked children so much was because they didn't think miracles were impossible. Nor did they doubt. Nor did they betray him.

They just believed, and that's what God wants all of us to do.

Long ago, a boy named Jeremiah lived in Israel. One day he heard a voice saying, **"Before I formed you in the womb I knew you. Before you were born I set you apart. I appointed you as a prophet to the nations."**

But Jeremiah had no idea how that could be the case, for he was very young.

"Ah, Lord God!" Jeremiah said. **"Truly I do not know how to speak, for I am only a boy."**

God thought differently.

"Do not say, 'I am only a boy,' for you shall go to all to whom I send you, and you shall speak whatever I command. Do not be afraid of them, for I am with you."

Just as with Jeremiah, God has important work for you to do, right now. God might want you to use your gifts in art or music or writing to make the world a more beautiful place. God might want you to visit a sick neighbor or to help make meals for hungry children in a faraway land. Someday, God might want you to teach or fight fires or raise children.

The important thing is to listen for God's voice—and to act on it when you hear it. At church, we often say these words at the end of the service: "Send us out into the world to do the work you have given us to do."

What work has God given you to do?

Reflection Questions:

- Who was your favorite character in these stories? What did you like about her or him?

- What was surprising or exciting to you about these Bible stories?

- What did you wonder about while hearing these stories?

- What work has God given you to do?

Resources

If you have enjoyed *The Path: Family Storybook* then we have great news: this is only the beginning! *The Path: Family Storybook* features twenty-four stories, selected to tell the overarching narrative of the Bible. But these are not all (or even most!) of the wonderful stories in the Bible. There is so much more to read and discover about God's story of love for all of us.

If you want to keep reading, there are some suggestions below for Bibles that do a great job of continuing the journey. They will contain many of the stories that you have read and loved in *The Path: Family Storybook*. But there will also be new and wonderful stories of God's love that we didn't have room to include here. If you have younger children or are looking for more stories that are easy to read and understand, then it would be best to start with one of the Storybook Bibles. Like *The Path: Family Storybook*, these include stories that are adapted to be especially accessible to kids. They also include some beautiful illustrations that bring the stories to life.

Then, when you and your family are ready, move on to a complete children's Bible. These books include the full text of the Bible. The ones suggested below also have helpful boxes and sidebars with additional information, reflection questions, and action points. Storybook Bibles are a great start, but there is no substitute for reading the whole story of the Bible, the epic of God's great love for us. So continue your family's journey with the Bible, and discover all that God has in store for you!

Suggested Storybook Bibles

- *The Bible for Children* by Murray Watts. Good Books, 2002.

- *The Jesus Storybook Bible: Every Story Whispers His Name* by Sally-Lloyd Jones. ZonderKidz, 2007.

- *The Spark Story Bible: Spark a Journey Through God's Word.* Sparkhouse Family, 2015.

- *The Family Story Bible* by Ralph Milton. Westminster John Knox Press, 1997.

Suggested Children's Bibles

- *Kids Spark NRSV Bible.* Augsburg Fortress Publishers, 2009.

- *CEB Deep Blue Kids Bible.* Common English Bible, 2015.

- *NIrV, Adventure Bible for Early Readers.* ZonderKidz, 2014. and NIV Adventure Bible. ZonderKidz, 2013.

About the Authors

Lindsay Hardin Freeman is a Minnesota-based Episcopal priest, author, and mother. She has won over thirty awards for journalistic excellence and is the author and/or editor of eight books, including *Bible Women: All Their Words and Why They Matter*, published by Forward Movement, and *The Scarlet Cord: Conversations with God's Chosen Women*. She also has written two children's books, *The Spy on Noah's Ark and Other Bible Stories from the Inside Out* and *Meet the Saints: Family Storybook*, published by Forward Movement. She is married to Leonard Freeman, a poet, priest, and teacher, and has two sons and four stepchildren.

Melody Wilson Shobe is an Episcopal priest who has served churches in Rhode Island and Texas. A graduate of Tufts University and Virginia Theological Seminary, Melody is currently working on curriculum development for Forward Movement. She served as the editor for *The Path: A Journey through the Bible* and is a coauthor of *Transforming Questions*, both published by Forward Movement. Melody, her husband, and their two daughters live in Dallas, Texas, where she spends her spare time reading stories, building forts, conquering playgrounds, baking cookies, and exploring nature.

About the Illustrator

Roger Speer is a lifelong servant of The Episcopal Church. He has served with mission, congregational, diocesan, national, and international formation initiatives during an exciting tenure as a youth minister. At heart, Roger is an artist and craftsman. He holds degrees in art education and graphic design, as well as various training certifications that he uses to produce new ways to express the gospel with as much innovation as possible. He is husband to Fran and father to Fynn.

The images are available as coloring pages in *Pathways of Faith*, an all-ages coloring book, available at www.ForwardMovement.org.

About Forward Movement

Forward Movement is committed to inspiring disciples and empowering evangelists. While we produce great resources like this storybook, Forward Movement is not a publishing company. We are a ministry.

Our mission is to support you in your spiritual journey, to help you grow as a follower of Jesus Christ. Publishing books, daily reflections, studies for small groups, and online resources is an important way that we live out this ministry. More than a half million people read our daily devotions through *Forward Day by Day,* which is also available in Spanish (*Adelante Día a Día*) and Braille, online, as a podcast, and as an app for your smartphones or tablets. It is mailed to more than fifty countries, and we donate nearly 30,000 copies each quarter to prisons, hospitals, and nursing homes. We actively seek partners across the Church and look for ways to provide resources that inspire and challenge.

A ministry of the Episcopal Church for more than eighty years, Forward Movement is a nonprofit organization funded by sales of resources and gifts from generous donors. To learn more about Forward Movement and our resources, please visit us at www.ForwardMovement.org (or www.VenAdelante.org).

We are delighted to be doing this work and invite your prayers and support.

CPSIA information can be obtained
at www.ICGtesting.com
Printed in the USA
LVOW02s1011230217

525187LV00007B/289/P